HEINEMANN MODULAR MATHEMATICS
for
EDEXCEL AS AND A-LEVEL

Revise for Mechanics 3

John Hebborn Jean Littlewood

Heinemann

Edexcel
Success through qualifications

Heinemann Educational Publishers,
a division of Heinemann Publishers (Oxford) Ltd,
Halley Court, Jordan Hill, Oxford, OX2 8EJ

OXFORD MELBOURNE AUCKLAND JOHANNESBURG
BLANTYRE GABORONE PORTSMOUTH NH (USA) CHICAGO

First published 2002

04 03 02
10 9 8 7 6 5 4 3 2

ISBN 0 435 51115 7

Cover design by Gecko Limited

Original design by Geoffrey Wadsley; additional design work by Jim Turner

Typeset and illustrated by Tech-Set Limited, Gateshead, Tyne and Wear

Printed in Great Britain by Scotprint, Haddington

Acknowledgements:

The publisher's and authors' thanks are due to Edexcel for permission to reproduce questions from past examination papers. These are marked with an [E].

The answers have been provided by the authors and are not the responsibility of the examining board.

About this book

This book is designed to help you get your best possible grade in your Mechanics 3 examination. The authors are Chief and Principal examiners and moderators, and have a good understanding of Edexcel's requirements.

Revise for Mechanics 3 covers the key topics that are tested in the Mechanics 3 exam paper. You can use this book to help you revise at the end of your course, or you can use it throughout your course alongside the course textbook, *Heinemann Modular Mathematics for Edexcel AS and A-level Mechanics 3*, which provides complete coverage of the syllabus.

Helping you prepare for your exam

To help you prepare, each topic offers you:

- **Key points to remember** – summarise the mathematical ideas you need to know and be able to use.
- **Worked examples and examination questions** – help you understand and remember important methods, and show you how to set out your answers clearly.
- **Revision exercises** – help you practise using these important methods to solve problems. Exam-level questions are included so you can be sure you are reaching the right standard, and answers are given at the back of the book so you can assess your progress.
- **Test yourself questions** – help you see where you need extra revision and practice. If you do need extra help they show you where to look in the *Heinemann Modular Mathematics for Edexcel AS and A-level Mechanics 3* textbook.

Exam practice and advice on revising

Examination style paper – this paper at the end of the book provides a set of questions of examination standard. It gives you an opportunity to practise taking a complete exam before you meet the real thing. The answers are given at the back of the book.

How to revise – for advice on revising before the exam, read the How to revise section on the next page.

How to revise using this book

Making the best use of your revision time

The topics in this book have been arranged in a logical sequence so you can work your way through them from beginning to end. But **how** you work on them depends on how much time there is between now and your examination.

If you have plenty of time before the exam then you can **work through each topic in turn**, covering the key points and worked examples before doing the revision exercises and Test yourself questions.

If you are short of time then you can **work through the Test yourself sections first**, to help you see which topics you need to do further work on.

However much time you have to revise, make sure you break your revision into short blocks of about 40 minutes, separated by five- or ten-minute breaks. Nobody can study effectively for hours without a break.

Using the Test yourself sections

Each Test yourself section provides a set of key questions. Try each question:

- If you can do it and get the correct answer then move on to the next topic. Come back to this topic later to consolidate your knowledge and understanding by working through the key points, worked examples and revision exercises.
- If you cannot do the question, or get an incorrect answer or part answer, then work through the key points, worked examples and revision exercises before trying the Test yourself questions again. If you need more help, the cross-references beside each Test yourself question show you where to find relevant information in the *Heinemann Modular Maths for Edexcel AS and A-level Mechanics 3* textbook.

Reviewing the key points

Most of the key points are straightforward ideas that you can learn: try to understand each one. Imagine explaining each idea to a friend in your own words, and say it out loud as you do so. This is a better way of making the ideas stick than just reading them silently from the page.

As you work through the book, remember to go back over key points from earlier topics at least once a week. This will help you to remember them in the exam.

Further kinematics

1

Key points to remember

1 For a particle P travelling in a straight line, which at time t seconds has a displacement x metres from a fixed point O of the line, the acceleration $a\,\mathrm{m\,s^{-2}}$ and the velocity $v\,\mathrm{m\,s^{-1}}$ as functions of time are given by:

$$a = \frac{dv}{dt}$$

$$v = \frac{dx}{dt}$$

$$a = \frac{d^2x}{dt^2}$$

2 When the acceleration is a function of the displacement then:

$$a = v\frac{dv}{dx} = \frac{d}{dx}\left(\frac{1}{2}v^2\right)$$

Example 1

A particle starts from rest and its acceleration after t seconds is:

$$\tfrac{1}{10}(18 + 3t - t^2)\,\mathrm{m\,s^{-2}}$$

until the acceleration becomes zero. After this instant the particle moves with the constant speed it has then reached. Find:

(a) the time taken to reach the particle's greatest speed

(b) the greatest speed

(c) the distance travelled by the particle in the first minute.

Answer

(a) The acceleration $a\,\mathrm{m\,s^{-2}}$ and the velocity $v\,\mathrm{m\,s^{-1}}$ are related by:

$$a = \frac{dv}{dt}$$

Using **1**

The maximum speed therefore occurs when $a = 0$.

So: $\frac{1}{10}(18 + 3t - t^2) = 0$

or: $(6 - t)(3 + t) = 0$

$\Rightarrow$ $t = 6$ or $t = -3$

But $t \geqslant 0$, so $t = 6$.

The time taken to reach the particle's greatest speed is 6 seconds.

(b) Since $a = \dfrac{dv}{dt}$

$$v = \int a\,dt$$
$$= \frac{1}{10}\int (18 + 3t - t^2)\,dt$$
$$= \frac{1}{10}\left(18t + \frac{3t^2}{2} - \frac{t^3}{3}\right) + c$$

As the particle starts from rest:

$$v = 0 \text{ when } t = 0 \text{ so } c = 0$$

and: $$v = \frac{1}{10}\left(18t + \frac{3t^2}{2} - \frac{t^3}{3}\right)$$

The greatest speed, when $t = 6$, is:

$$v = \frac{1}{10}\left\{18 \times 6 + \left[\frac{3}{2} \times (6)^2\right] - \frac{(6)^3}{3}\right\}$$
$$= \frac{1}{10}\left[108 + \left(\frac{3}{2} \times 36\right) - \frac{216}{3}\right]$$
$$= 9$$

So the greatest speed is $9\,\text{m}\,\text{s}^{-1}$.

(c) The distance travelled is obtained from $\dfrac{ds}{dt} = v$.

Using **1**

So: $$s = \int v\,dt$$
$$= \frac{1}{10}\int\left(18t + \frac{3}{2}t^2 - \frac{1}{3}t^3\right)dt$$
$$= \frac{1}{10}\left[\left(18 \times \frac{t^2}{2}\right) + \left(\frac{3}{2} \times \frac{t^3}{3}\right) - \left(\frac{1}{3} \times \frac{t^4}{4}\right)\right] + k$$

Taking $s = 0$ at $t = 0$ gives $k = 0$.

So: $$s = \frac{1}{10}\left(9t^2 + \frac{t^3}{2} - \frac{t^4}{12}\right)$$

When the particle reaches its greatest speed, $t = 6$ and the distance travelled is:

The result obtained in **(a)**.

$$s = \tfrac{1}{10}\left\{[9 \times (6)^2] + \frac{(6)^3}{2} - \frac{6^4}{12}\right\}$$
$$= \tfrac{1}{10}(324 + 108 - 108)$$
$$= 32.4\,\text{m}$$

For the remaining $(60 - 6) = 54$ seconds of the first minute the particle travels with a constant speed of $9\,\text{m}\,\text{s}^{-1}$ and covers a distance of $9 \times 54\,\text{m}$.

The result obtained in **(b)**.

Total distance travelled in first minute is then
$(32.4 + 486)\,\text{m} = 518.4\,\text{m}$.

Example 2

A particle P, moving along a straight line, starts at time $t = 0$ seconds with a velocity of $4\,\text{m}\,\text{s}^{-1}$. At any subsequent time the acceleration of P is $(6t - 8)\,\text{m}\,\text{s}^{-2}$.
Find:

(a) the distance travelled by P before it first comes to instantaneous rest
(b) the total time, T seconds, taken by P to return to the starting point
(c) the greatest speed of P for $0 \leqslant t \leqslant T$.

Answer

(**a**) Since $a = 6t - 8$

$$v = \int a\,\text{d}t$$
$$= \int (6t - 8)\,\text{d}t$$
$$= \left(6 \times \frac{t^2}{2}\right) - 8t + c$$

Using **1**

$v = 4$ when $t = 0$ so $c = 4$

and: $v = 3t^2 - 8t + 4$

P comes to instantaneous rest when $v = 0$.

So: $$3t^2 - 8t + 4 = 0$$
$$(3t - 2)(t - 2) = 0$$
$$\Rightarrow \quad t = \tfrac{2}{3} \text{ or } t = 2$$

P **first** comes to instantaneous rest when $t = \frac{2}{3}$.

Since: $v = \frac{ds}{dt}$

Using **1**

$$s = \int v\,dt = \int (3t^2 - 8t + 4)\,dt$$

$$= \left(3 \times \frac{t^3}{3}\right) - \left(8 \times \frac{t^2}{2}\right) + 4t + k$$

Taking $s = 0$ when $t = 0$ gives $k = 0$, so:

$$s = t^3 - 4t^2 + 4t$$

When $t = \frac{2}{3}$ the distance travelled is:

$$\left(\frac{2}{3}\right)^3 - 4\left(\frac{2}{3}\right)^2 + 4\left(\frac{2}{3}\right)$$

$$= \frac{32}{27}$$

$$= 1\tfrac{5}{27}$$

So the distance P travels before it first comes instantaneously to rest is $1\frac{5}{27}$ m.

(b) P returns to the starting point when $s = 0$.

So: $t^3 - 4t^2 + 4t = 0$

or: $t(t^2 - 4t + 4) = 0$

$t(t-2)^2 = 0$

so: $t = 0$ or $t = 2$

P takes 2 seconds to return to the starting point.

(c) To find the greatest speed of P you should draw a sketch of v against t.

We have: $v = 4$ when $t = 0$

$v = 0$ when $t = \frac{2}{3}$ and $t = 2$

and v is a quadratic function of t. The graph opens upwards as $v = 3t^2 - 8t + 4$.

Positive coefficient of t^2 so graph opens upwards.

A sketch of v against t is then:

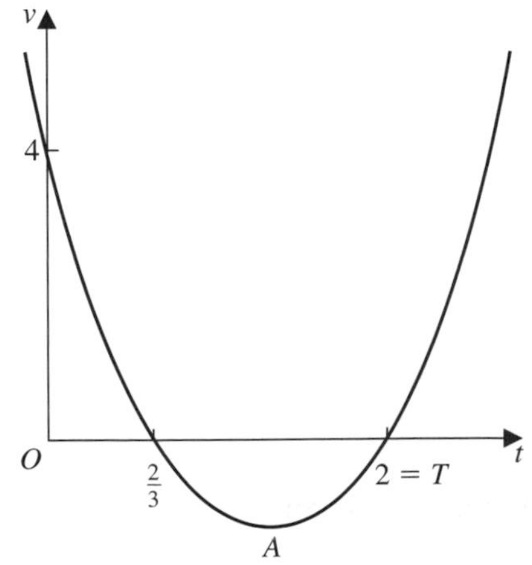

The minimum point A on the curve occurs when $t = \frac{1}{2}(2 + \frac{2}{3})$, by symmetry, so $t = 1\frac{1}{3}$.

Alternatively, a minimum occurs when $a = 0$, so $6t - 8 = 0$ and $t = 1\frac{1}{3}$.

When $t = 1\frac{1}{3}$, $v = 3\left(\frac{4}{3}\right)^2 - 8\left(\frac{4}{3}\right) + 4$

$$= -1\tfrac{1}{3}$$

Hence the greatest speed of P actually occurs when $t = 0$, when the speed is $4\,\text{m s}^{-1}$.

Example 3

A particle moves along a horizontal straight line with acceleration proportional to $\cos \pi t$ where t seconds is the time.

When $t = 0$, the speed of the particle is $u\,\text{m s}^{-1}$ and when $t = \frac{1}{2}$ its speed is $2u\,\text{m s}^{-1}$.

Find the distance, in m, the particle has travelled when $t = 2$ and draw a speed–time graph for $0 \leqslant t \leqslant 2$.

Answer

Let acceleration $a = k \cos \pi t$, where k is a constant, then

$$\frac{\mathrm{d}v}{\mathrm{d}t} = k \cos \pi t.$$

Using **1**

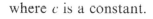

Integrating with respect to t gives:

$$v = \frac{k}{\pi} \sin \pi t + c$$

where c is a constant.

Since $v = u$ when $t = 0$

Recall $\sin 0 = 0$.

$\Rightarrow$ $c = u$

So: $v = \dfrac{k}{\pi} \sin \pi t + u$

Since $v = 2u$ when $t = \frac{1}{2}$

$$2u = \frac{k}{\pi} \sin\left(\frac{\pi}{2}\right) + u$$

or: $u = \dfrac{k}{\pi}$

Recall $\sin\left(\frac{\pi}{2}\right) = 1$.

So: $k = \pi u$

and: $v = u \sin \pi t + u$ (1)

To find the distance travelled we use $v = \dfrac{ds}{dt}$.

Using **1**

So: $s = \displaystyle\int v\,dt = \int (u \sin \pi t + u)\,dt$

$$= -\frac{u}{\pi}\cos \pi t + ut + A \text{ where } A \text{ is a constant.}$$

Taking $s = 0$ when $t = 0$ gives:

$$-\frac{u}{\pi} + A = 0 \Rightarrow A = \frac{u}{\pi}$$

Recall $\cos 0 = 1$.

So:

$$s = -\frac{u}{\pi}\cos \pi t + ut + \frac{u}{\pi}$$

When $t = 2$

$$s = -\frac{u}{\pi}\cos 2\pi + 2u + \frac{u}{\pi} = 2u$$

Recall $\cos 2\pi = 1$.

So distance travelled when $t = 2$ is $2u$ metres.

From (1) the speed–time graph is a sine curve shifted upwards by u.

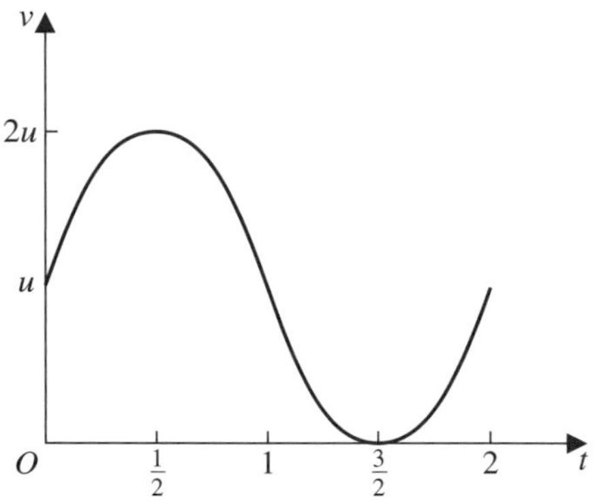

Example 4

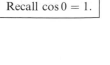

A particle moves on the positive x-axis. When its displacement from O is x metres its acceleration is of magnitude $\dfrac{k^2}{x^3}$ m s^{-2}, where k is a positive constant, and directed towards O. Initially, when $t = 0$ the particle is at rest and $x = 1$. Find the time the particle takes to reach $x = \frac{1}{2}$.

Answer

As the acceleration is a function of the displacement we have:

$$a = v\frac{dv}{dx} = \frac{d}{dx}\left(\tfrac{1}{2}v^2\right)$$

Using **2**

$$= -\frac{k^2}{x^3}$$

Note negative sign because acceleration is towards O.

Integrating with respect to x:

$$\tfrac{1}{2}v^2 = -\int \frac{k^2}{x^3}\,dx$$

$$= \frac{k^2}{2x^2} + c \text{ where } c \text{ is a constant.}$$

As $v = 0$ when $x = 1$:

$$0 = \frac{k^2}{2} + c$$

So: $$c = -\frac{k^2}{2}$$

and: $$v^2 = \frac{k^2}{x^2} - k^2 = k^2\left(\frac{1}{x^2} - 1\right)$$

To find the time taken use $v = \frac{ds}{dt}$.

Using **1**

From above, $v = \pm k\left(\frac{1}{x^2} - 1\right)^{\frac{1}{2}}$.

Initially, when $t = 0$ and $x = 1$ the speed is zero but the acceleration is **towards** O so the negative square root is required.

So: $$\frac{dx}{dt} = -\frac{k}{x}(1 - x^2)^{\frac{1}{2}}$$

or: $$-\int \frac{x\,dx}{(1 - x^2)^{\frac{1}{2}}} = k\int dt$$

So: $$-\int x(1 - x^2)^{-\frac{1}{2}}\,dx = k\int dt$$

Integrating: $$(1 - x^2)^{\frac{1}{2}} = kt + A$$

As $x = 1$ when $t = 0$, the constant A is zero.

So: $$t = \frac{1}{k}(1 - x^2)^{\frac{1}{2}}$$

When $x = \frac{1}{2}$:

$$t = \frac{1}{k}\left[1 - \left(\frac{1}{2}\right)^2\right]^{\frac{1}{2}}$$

$$= \frac{1}{k}\left(\frac{3}{4}\right)^{\frac{1}{2}}$$

$$= \frac{1}{2k}\sqrt{3}$$

So the particle takes $\frac{1}{2k}\sqrt{3}$ seconds to reach $x = \frac{1}{2}$.

Example 5

O is a fixed point on a straight line on which a particle P moves. The acceleration of P when its displacement from O is x m is $(8 - 4x)\,\text{m s}^{-2}$. When $x = 2$ the speed of P is $6\,\text{m s}^{-1}$.

(a) Obtain an expression for the speed $v\,\text{m s}^{-1}$ of P when the displacement is x m.

(b) Hence determine the values of x for which the speed is zero.

Answer

(a) For the given acceleration:

$$\ddot{x} = \frac{\mathrm{d}}{\mathrm{d}x}\left(\tfrac{1}{2}v^2\right) = 8 - 4x$$

Using **2**

Integrating with respect to x:

$$\tfrac{1}{2}v^2 = \int (8 - 4x)\,\mathrm{d}x = 8x - \left(4 \times \frac{x^2}{2}\right) + c$$

Since $v = 6$ when $x = 2$:

$$\begin{aligned} c &= \tfrac{1}{2}(36) - (8 \times 2) + [2 \times (2)^2] \\ &= 18 - 16 + 8 \\ &= 10 \end{aligned}$$

So: $$v^2 = 16x - 4x^2 + 20$$

(b) The speed is zero when $16x - 4x^2 + 20 = 0$, or:

$$\begin{aligned} x^2 - 4x - 5 &= 0 \\ (x - 5)(x + 1) &= 0 \\ x = -1 \text{ or } x &= 5 \end{aligned}$$

Revision exercise 1

1 A particle starts from rest at time $t = 0$ and moves in a straight line with variable acceleration $f\,\text{m s}^{-2}$ where

$$f = \tfrac{1}{5}(20 - 3t) \qquad (0 \leqslant t \leqslant 5)$$

$$f = \frac{t}{5} \qquad (5 \leqslant t \leqslant 10)$$

t being measured in seconds.

(a) Show that when $t = 10$ the speed of the particle is $20\,\text{m s}^{-1}$.

(b) Find, to the nearest metre, the distance travelled by the particle in the first 10 seconds.

2 A particle P moves in a straight line Ox so that at time t seconds its acceleration in the direction of x increasing is $8te^{2t}$ m s^{-2}. Given that P starts from rest at O when $t = 0$, find:

(a) the speed of P when $t = \frac{1}{2}$

(b) the distance of P from O when $t = \frac{1}{2}$.

3 A particle moves from rest at a point O along a straight line Ox. At time t seconds its acceleration is inversely proportional to $(1 + t)$ in the direction of x increasing. Given that after time T its speed is U, show that after a time t its distance s from O will be given by:

$$s \ln(1 + T) = U[(1 + t)\ln(1 + t) - t]$$

4 A particle P moves along the line Ox. When its displacement from O is x metres, its acceleration is of magnitude $\dfrac{10}{x^2}$ m s^{-2} and directed towards O. Given that when $x = 5$ the speed of P is 6 m s^{-1} towards O, find v, the speed of P, when $x = 2$.

5 The acceleration of a particle P moving on the line Ox is $k(2x + 1)$ m s^{-2}, when P has a displacement x metres from O. The acceleration is away from O. Given that when $x = 0$ the speed of P is 1 m s^{-1} and when $x = 3$ the speed of P is 7 m s^{-1}, find the value of k.

6 A particle P moves along a straight line and when its distance from a fixed point O is x metres its retardation is $(7 + 2x)$ m s^{-2}. Given that the speed of P is 6 m s^{-1} when $x = 0$, obtain an expression for the speed v in terms of x. Find the value of x when P comes to rest.

7 A particle P moves along the x-axis with acceleration away from the origin O inversely proportional to OP^2. It is initially at rest with $OP = a$ and when $OP = 2a$ its velocity is V.

(a) Show that when $OP = x$ the speed v of P is given by $v^2 = 2V^2\left(1 - \dfrac{a}{x}\right)$.

(b) Show also that when $OP = ka$, where k is large, the speed of P is approximately $(2k - 1)V/(k\sqrt{2})$.

8 When a particle P has a displacement x metres from O, a fixed point in a straight line, its acceleration is $\lambda\left(x+\frac{a^4}{x^3}\right)$, where $\lambda > 0$, towards O. Given that P starts from rest when $x = a$:

(a) find the speed v of P as a function of x

(b) show that the time taken to reach O is $\pi/(4\sqrt{\lambda})$

(c) find the time taken to reach the point $a/\sqrt{2}$ from a.

Test yourself | What to review

If your answer is incorrect:

1 On joining a major road a car accelerates for 10 s from a speed of 20 m s^{-1} to reach a top speed of 35 m s^{-1}. In an initial model of the situation, the acceleration is assumed to be constant.

(a) Estimate the distance, in m, travelled by the car during this 10 s period.

It is noticed that the acceleration of the car decreases as its speed increases. A refined model is proposed in which the acceleration of the car t seconds after it starts to accelerate is taken to be $k(10 - t)$, $0 \leqslant t \leqslant 10$, where k is a positive constant.

(b) Find the value of k.

(c) Find a revised estimate for the distance, in m, travelled by the car during the 10 s period.

Review Heinemann Book M3 pages 1–12

---

2 A particle moves along the positive x-axis. When it has a displacement of x metres from O its acceleration is of magnitude $\frac{9}{x^3}$ m s^{-2} and is directed towards O. Given that initially, when $t = 0$, the velocity of the particle is 3 m s^{-1} in the direction Ox and $x = 1$, find:

(a) velocity v as a function of x

(b) x as a function of t.

Review Heinemann Book M3 pages 14–18

Test yourself answers

1 **(a)** 275 m **(b)** $k = \frac{3}{10}$ **(c)** 300 m

2 **(a)** $v = \frac{3}{x}$ **(b)** $x = \sqrt{6t+1}$

Elastic springs and strings

2

Key points to remember

1 Elastic springs and strings have a tension, T, given by:

$$T = \frac{\lambda x}{l}$$

where λ is the modulus of elasticity, x is the extension and l is the natural length of the spring or string. This is known as Hooke's law.

2 An elastic spring may be compressed by a length x. The thrust in a compressed spring is also given by Hooke's law.

3 The work done in stretching (or compressing) an elastic string (or spring) with modulus λ from its natural length l to a length $(l + x)$ (or $(l - x)$) is $\frac{\lambda x^2}{2l}$.

4 The elastic potential energy (E.P.E.) in a spring or string of modulus λ extended or compressed by a length x beyond its natural length is also $\frac{\lambda x^2}{2l}$.

5 The total change in the mechanical energies (that is kinetic, gravitational potential and elastic potential energies) of a system is equal to the work done by any external forces acting on the system.

Worked examination question 1 [E]

A light elastic string of natural length 0.3 m has one end fixed to a point on a ceiling. To the other end of the string is attached a particle of mass M. When the particle is hanging in equilibrium, the length of the string is 0.4 m.

(a) Determine, in terms of M and g, the modulus of elasticity of the string.

A horizontal force is applied to the particle so that it is held in equilibrium with the string making an angle α with the downward vertical. The length of the string is now 0.45 m.

(b) Find α, to the nearest degree.

Answer

(a)

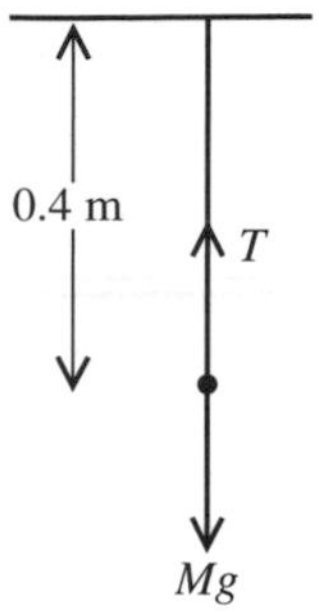

Resolving $\uparrow$: $T - Mg = 0$

The particle is in equilibrium.

Using **1**: $T = \dfrac{\lambda x}{l}$ with $l = 0.3$ and $x = 0.1$ gives:

$$T = \frac{\lambda \times 0.1}{0.3}$$

So: $$Mg = \frac{\lambda \times 0.1}{0.3} = \frac{\lambda}{3}$$

$\Rightarrow$ $$\lambda = 3Mg$$

(b) Using **1**: $T_1 = \dfrac{\lambda x}{l}$ with $l = 0.3$ and $x = 0.15$ gives:

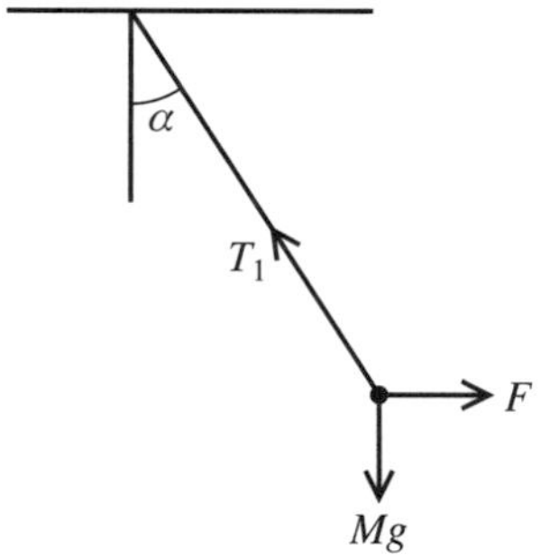

$$T_1 = 3Mg \times \frac{0.15}{0.3} = \frac{3Mg}{2}$$

Resolving $\uparrow$: $T_1 \cos\alpha - Mg = 0$

So: $$\cos\alpha = \frac{Mg}{\frac{3Mg}{2}} = \frac{2}{3}$$

$$\alpha = 48.1^\circ = 48^\circ$$

The answer was required to the nearest degree.

Example 1

A uniform rod AB of mass M and length $2l$ is smoothly hinged to a vertical wall at A. It is held in equilibrium, at an angle of 60° to the upward vertical, by a light elastic string of natural length $2l$. One end of the string is attached to point C of the rod, where $AC = \frac{3}{2}l$, and the other end is attached to point D of the wall, vertically above A, where $AD = \frac{3}{2}l$. Find, in terms of M and g, the modulus of elasticity of the string.

Answer

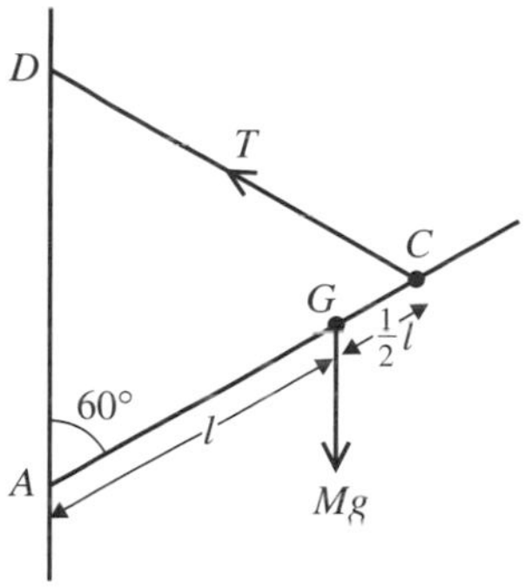

Taking moments about A:

$$T \times \tfrac{3}{2}l\cos 30^\circ - Mgl\cos 30^\circ = 0$$

So: $$T = \tfrac{2}{3}Mg \qquad (1)$$

Taking moments about A produces an equation which does not involve the unknown reaction at A.

$\triangle ACD$ is isosceles and $\angle CAD = 60^\circ$ so $\triangle ACD$ is in fact equilateral. Hence $CD = \frac{3}{2}l$ and the extension in the string $= \frac{3}{2}l - l = \frac{1}{2}l$.

Using **1** : $T = \dfrac{\lambda x}{l}$ (2)

Using (1) and (2) gives: $$\tfrac{2}{3}Mg = \frac{\lambda \times \frac{l}{2}}{l} \Rightarrow \lambda = \tfrac{4}{3}Mg$$

Worked examination question 2 [E]

A light elastic string has natural length a and modulus λ. Find, in terms of a and λ, the work done in stretching the string from twice its natural length to three times its natural length.

Answer

Initial extension is a, so using **4**, the initial elastic potential energy (E.P.E.) is:

$$\frac{\lambda a^2}{2a} = \frac{\lambda a}{2}$$

You must consider the change in *energies*, not the change in length.

Final extension is $2a$, so using **4**,

final E.P.E. $= \dfrac{\lambda(2a)^2}{2a} = \dfrac{\lambda \times 4a^2}{2a} = 2\lambda a.$

Using **5**: work done $= 2\lambda a - \frac{1}{2}\lambda a = \frac{3}{2}\lambda a$

Worked examination question 3 [E]

One end of a light elastic string, of natural length d, is attached to a fixed point A. A particle P, of mass m, is attached at the other end of the string. The stretched string AP is of length $\frac{6}{5}d$ when P hangs in equilibrium vertically below A. The particle P is now held at A and projected vertically downwards with speed $\sqrt{(dg)}$.
Find, in terms of d, the distance of P below A when P first comes to instantaneous rest.

horizontal ceiling. The particle is pulled aside by a horizontal force S until the spring makes an angle of 40° with the vertical. Find the extension in the spring and the magnitude of S.

3 The ends of a light elastic string of natural length l are attached to points A and B of a horizontal ceiling where $AB = 2l$. A particle P of mass M is attached to the mid-point of the string and hangs in equilibrium at a distance $\frac{5}{12}l$ below the level of AB. Find, in terms of M and g, the modulus of elasticity of the string.

4 Two stretched elastic strings AB and CD, each of natural length 1 m, hang vertically from points on the same horizontal level and support horizontally a rod BD of mass 27 kg. The position of the centre of mass of the rod is G, where $BG:GD = 2:1$ and $AB = CD = 1.09$ m.
The moduli of elasticity of AB and CD are λ_1 and λ_2 respectively. Show that $\lambda_1 = 980$ N and calculate λ_2.
A mass of 18 kg is now attached to the mid-point of the rod, and the strings are arranged to remain vertical with AC horizontal. Calculate:

(a) the tension in each string

(b) the vertical difference in level of the ends of the rod BD, stating clearly which is the lower end. [E]

5

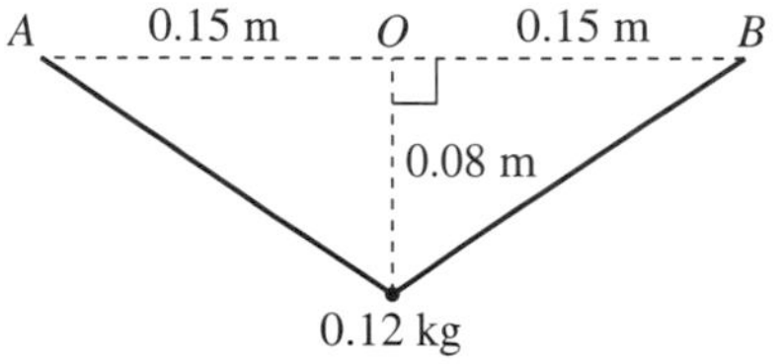

Two light elastic strings each have natural length 0.15 m and modulus 75 N. One end of each string is attached to a particle of mass 0.12 kg, and the other ends are attached to points A and B, 0.3 m apart at the same horizontal level. The particle is initially held at rest 0.08 m vertically below O, the mid-point of AB, as shown in the diagram.

(a) Find the tension in each of the elastic strings.

(b) Show that the energy stored in each of the strings is 0.1 J.

The particle is released from rest in this position, and subsequently passes through O with speed v metres per second.

(c) Use the principle of conservation of energy to calculate v, giving your answer to two significant figures. [E]

6 An elastic string, of natural length l and modulus of elasticity λ, is stretched to a length $l + x$. As a result, the tension in the string is mg and the energy stored in it is E. Find x and λ in terms of E, g, l and m. [E]

7 An elastic string, of natural length 2 m and modulus of elasticity 6 N, is stretched on a horizontal table by applying a force of magnitude 2 N. Find the extension of the string. Find also the work done in stretching the string from its natural length. [E]

8 One end of a light elastic string, of natural length a and modulus of elasticity $3mg$, is fixed at a point A and the other end carries a particle P of mass m. The particle is held at A and then projected vertically down with speed $\sqrt{(3ga)}$. Find the distance AP when the acceleration of the particle is instantaneously zero.
Find also the maximum speed attained by the particle during its motion. [E]

Test yourself

What to review

If your answer is incorrect:

1 One end of an elastic string of modulus of elasticity λ is attached to a point on a horizontal ceiling. When a particle of mass m hangs freely attached to the other end of the string, the length of the string is increased by 25%.
(a) Find λ, in terms of m and g.

If instead a particle of mass $3m$ hangs freely attached to the end of the string, the length of the string is 60 cm.
(b) Find the natural length of the string.

Review Heinemann Book M3 pages 24–28

---

2 A particle of mass 3 kg is attached to one end A of a light elastic spring of modulus of elasticity 80 N and natural length 1 m. The other end of the spring is attached to a fixed point B on a rough horizontal floor. The coefficient of friction between the particle and the floor is $\frac{1}{3}$.

Review Heinemann Book M3 pages 24–28 and pages 40–45

(a) Show that the particle can rest in equilibrium on the floor with $AB = 1.1$ m.

The particle is now pulled aside, without losing contact with the floor, until $AB = 1.3$ m and released from rest.
(b) Find the speed of the particle when the spring first returns to its natural length.

---

3 Prove that the elastic energy of a light spring of natural length a and modulus of elasticity λ, stretched by an amount x, is $\frac{\lambda x^2}{2a}$.

Review Heinemann Book M3 pages 37–38 and pages 40–45

A trolley of mass m runs down a smooth track of constant inclination $\frac{\pi}{6}$ to the horizontal, carrying at its front a light spring of natural length a and modulus $\frac{mga}{c}$, where c is constant. When the spring is fully compressed it is of length $\frac{a}{4}$, and it obeys Hooke's law up to this point. After the trolley has travelled a distance b from rest the spring meets a fixed stop. Show that, when the spring has been compressed a distance x, where $x < \frac{3a}{4}$, the speed v of the trolley is given by $\frac{cv^2}{g} = c(b + x) - x^2$.

Given that $c = \frac{a}{10}$ and $b = 2a$, find the total distance covered by the trolley before it momentarily comes to rest for the first time. [E]

Test yourself answers

1 **(a)** $\lambda = 4mg$ **(b)** $34\frac{2}{7}$ cm

2 **(b)** $0.663\ \text{m s}^{-1}$

3 $\frac{5a}{2}$

Further dynamics

3

Key points to remember

1 For a particle of mass m moving in a straight line under the influence of a force $F = \mathrm{F}(t)$

$$m\frac{\mathrm{d}v}{\mathrm{d}t} = \mathrm{F}(t)$$

2 For a particle of mass m moving in a straight line under the influence of a force $F = \mathrm{G}(x)$

$$m\frac{\mathrm{d}}{\mathrm{d}x}\left(\tfrac{1}{2}v^2\right) = \mathrm{G}(x)$$

3 The impulse of a variable force $\mathrm{F}(t)$ acting over the time interval t_1 to t_2

$$\int_{t_1}^{t_2} \mathrm{F}(t)\,\mathrm{d}t$$

4 The work done by a variable force $\mathrm{G}(x)$ which moves its point of application from x_1 to x_2 is:

$$\int_{x_1}^{x_2} \mathrm{G}(x)\,\mathrm{d}x$$

5 **The universal law of gravitation**
The force of attraction between two bodies of masses M_1 and M_2 is directly proportional to the product of their masses and inversely proportional to the square of the distance between them:

$$F = \frac{GM_1M_2}{d^2}$$

where G is a constant known as the constant of gravitation. This law is also known as Newton's law of gravitation.

6 A particle which moves on a straight line so that its acceleration is always towards a fixed point O in the line and is proportional to its displacement from O is said to be moving with simple harmonic motion (S.H.M.).

This is written as: $\ddot{x} = -\omega^2 x$

The maximum displacement of the particle from O is the amplitude, a, of the motion.

The period of the motion is $\frac{2\pi}{\omega}$.

The speed, v, at any point is given by:

$$v^2 = \omega^2(a^2 - x^2)$$

and $x = a \sin \omega t$ if $x = 0$ when $t = 0$

$x = a \cos \omega t$ if $x = a$ when $t = 0$

$x = a \sin(\omega t + \alpha)$ if x has some other value when $t = 0$

7 A particle attached to the end of an elastic spring which is displaced from its equilibrium position and then allowed to move under the influence of the tension or thrust only will move with S.H.M.
If the particle is attached to a string, the motion will be simple harmonic only while the string is taut.

Worked examination question 1 [E]

A particle P of mass 0.5 kg is moving in a horizontal plane under the action of a single variable force $\mathbf{F}$ newtons. At time t seconds, the velocity $\mathbf{v}$ m s^{-1} of P is given by:

$$\mathbf{v} = (-2\cos t)\mathbf{i} + t^2\mathbf{j}$$

where $\mathbf{i}$ and $\mathbf{j}$ are perpendicular unit vectors in the horizontal plane.

(a) Find the acceleration, $\mathbf{a}$ m s^{-2}, of P at time t seconds.

(b) Find the magnitude of $\mathbf{F}$ when $t = \frac{\pi}{2}$, giving your answer to two significant figures.

Answer

(a) $\mathbf{v} = (-2\cos t)\mathbf{i} + t^2\mathbf{j}$

$$\mathbf{a} = \frac{d\mathbf{v}}{dt} = 2\sin t\mathbf{i} + 2t\mathbf{j}$$

So the acceleration is $(2\sin t\mathbf{i} + 2t\mathbf{j})$ m s^{-2}.

(b) $\mathbf{F} = m\mathbf{a} \Rightarrow |\mathbf{F}| = m|\mathbf{a}|$

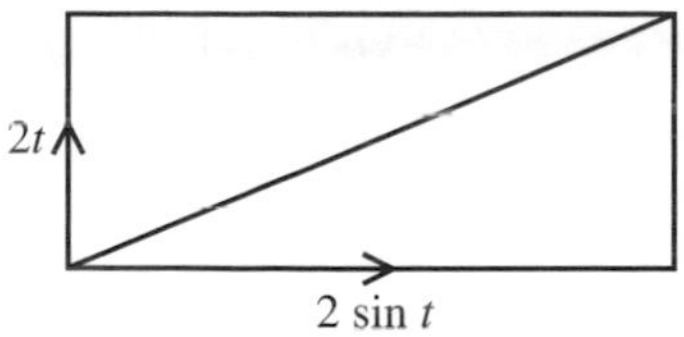

From **(a)**, $|\mathbf{a}| = \sqrt{[(2\sin t)^2 + (2t)^2]} = \sqrt{(4\sin^2 t + 4t^2)}$

The magnitude of a vector is its modulus.

When $t = \frac{\pi}{2}$, $|\mathbf{a}| = \sqrt{\left(4 + 4\frac{\pi^2}{4}\right)} = \sqrt{(4 + \pi^2)} = 3.72$

Hence $|\mathbf{F}| = m|\mathbf{a}| = 0.5 \times 3.72 = 1.9\,\text{N}$

The answer was required to two significant figures.

Example 1

A particle P of mass 0.2 kg is initially at rest on a smooth horizontal surface. A horizontal force of magnitude $(x^2 + 2)$ N, where x metres is the distance of P from its initial position, acts on the particle, causing it to move in a straight line. Calculate:

(a) the work done by the force in moving the particle 5 m from its initial position

(b) the speed of the particle when $x = 5$.

Answer

(a) Work done $= \int_0^5 (x^2 + 2)\,dx = \left[\frac{x^3}{3} + 2x\right]_0^5 = \frac{125}{3} + 10 - 0 = 51\frac{2}{3}$

Using **4**

Work done $= 51\frac{2}{3}$ J

(b) Work done = gain of K.E.

$$51\tfrac{2}{3} = \tfrac{1}{2}mv^2$$
$$\tfrac{155}{3} = \tfrac{1}{2} \times 0.2v^2$$

Initial speed = 0 so initial K.E. = 0.

So: $\quad v^2 = \frac{155}{3} \times \frac{2}{0.2}$

and: $\quad v = 22.7$

The speed of the particle is $22.7\,\text{m s}^{-1}$.

Example 2

A particle P of mass 0.4 kg is moving along the positive x-axis under the action of a force directed away from the origin O. At time t seconds after P leaves O the force has magnitude $(5 + 2t)$ N. When $t = 0$, P has speed $7\,\text{m s}^{-1}$. Calculate:

(a) the magnitude of the impulse given to P by the force between $t = 0$ and $t = 4$

(b) the speed of P when $t = 4$.

Answer

(a) Impulse $= \int F\,dt = \int_0^4 (5 + 2t)\,dt = \left[5t + t^2\right]_0^4 = 20 + 16$

Using **3**

The magnitude of the impulse is 36 N s.

(b) $I = mv - mu$

$36 = 0.4v - 0.4 \times 7$

Initial speed is $7\,\text{m}\,\text{s}^{-1}$.

So: $0.4v = 36 + 2.8$

and: $v = \frac{38.8}{0.4} = 97$

The speed of P is $97\,\text{m}\,\text{s}^{-1}$.

Worked examination question 2 [E]

A particle P moves in a straight line so that at time t seconds its distance x metres from a fixed point O in the line is given by:

$$x = 5\sin\left(\frac{\pi t}{6}\right)$$

(a) Find the acceleration of P at time t seconds and deduce that P is moving with simple harmonic motion.
(b) Write down the period and the amplitude of the motion of P.
(c) Calculate the time, in s, taken by P to move directly from O to the point A, where $OA = 2.5\,\text{m}$.

Answer

(a) $x = 5\sin\left(\frac{\pi t}{6}\right)$

$$\Rightarrow \dot{x} = 5\frac{\pi}{6}\cos\left(\frac{\pi t}{6}\right)$$

and $\ddot{x} = -5\frac{\pi^2}{36}\sin\left(\frac{\pi t}{6}\right) = -\frac{\pi^2}{36}x$

$\ddot{x}$ is the acceleration of P.

This equation is of the form $\ddot{x} = -\omega^2 x$.
Hence P is moving with S.H.M.

(b) $\ddot{x} = -\frac{\pi^2}{36}x$, so $\omega = \frac{\pi}{6}$

Period $= \frac{2\pi}{\omega} = 2\pi \times \frac{6}{\pi} = 12\,\text{s}$

$x = 5\sin\left(\frac{\pi t}{6}\right)$, so x is maximum when $\sin\left(\frac{\pi t}{6}\right)$ is maximum, that is when $\sin\left(\frac{\pi t}{6}\right) = 1$.

The maximum value of x is the amplitude.

Hence amplitude $= 5\,\text{m}$.

(c) As $OA = 2.5$, we need to find the time when $x = 2.5$.

$$2.5 = 5\sin\left(\frac{\pi t}{6}\right)$$

$$0.5 = \sin\left(\frac{\pi t}{6}\right)$$

So: $\frac{\pi}{6} = \frac{\pi t}{6}$

$\arcsin 0.5 = \frac{\pi}{6}$

and: $t = 1$

P takes 1 s to move directly from O to A.

Worked examination question 3 [E]

One end of a light elastic spring of natural length l is fixed to a point O. A particle P, of mass m, is attached at the other end of the spring and hangs in equilibrium at a distance $\frac{7l}{5}$ below O.

(a) Find, in terms of m and g, the modulus of elasticity of the spring.

The particle P is pulled down a further distance $\frac{l}{5}$ from its equilibrium position and released from rest. At time t after P is released the length of the spring is $x + \frac{7l}{5}$.

(b) Find a differential equation for the motion of P relating x and t and deduce that P is moving with simple harmonic motion.

Giving your answers in terms of l and g, find:

(c) the period of the motion of P

(d) the greatest speed of P.

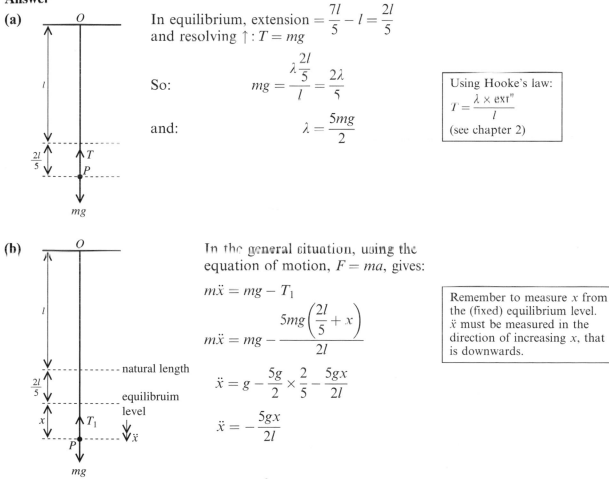

Answer

(a)

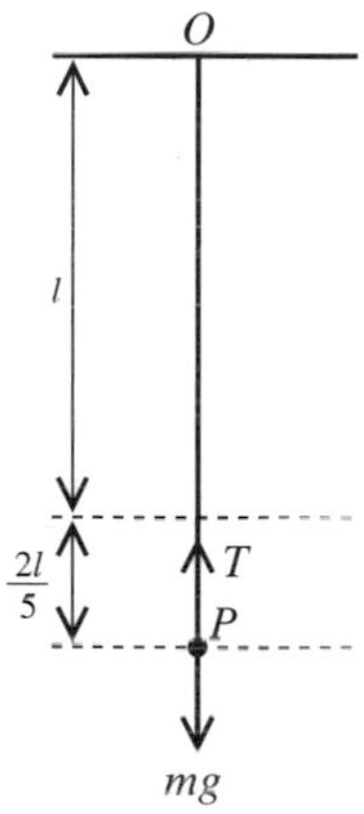

In equilibrium, extension $= \frac{7l}{5} - l = \frac{2l}{5}$
and resolving $\uparrow$: $T = mg$

So: $$mg = \frac{\lambda \frac{2l}{5}}{l} = \frac{2\lambda}{5}$$

and: $$\lambda = \frac{5mg}{2}$$

Using Hooke's law:
$T = \frac{\lambda \times \text{ext}^n}{l}$
(see chapter 2)

(b)

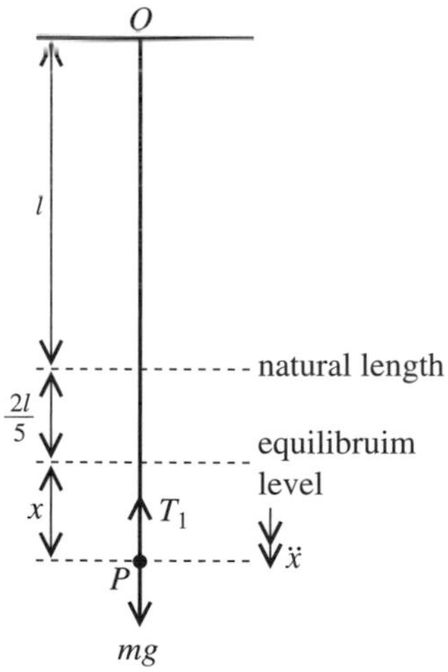

In the general situation, using the equation of motion, $F = ma$, gives:

$$m\ddot{x} = mg - T_1$$

$$m\ddot{x} = mg - \frac{5mg\left(\frac{2l}{5} + x\right)}{2l}$$

$$\ddot{x} = g - \frac{5g}{2} \times \frac{2}{5} - \frac{5gx}{2l}$$

$$\ddot{x} = -\frac{5gx}{2l}$$

Remember to measure x from the (fixed) equilibrium level. $\ddot{x}$ must be measured in the direction of increasing x, that is downwards.

As this equation is of the form $\ddot{x} = -\omega^2 x$, the particle is moving with S.H.M.

(c) Since $\ddot{x} = -\dfrac{5gx}{2l}$, $\omega = \sqrt{\left(\dfrac{5g}{2l}\right)}$

And so the period is $2\pi\sqrt{\left(\dfrac{2l}{5g}\right)}$

Using **6**

(d) To find the greatest speed use **6**: $v^2 = \omega^2(a^2 - x^2)$.

Maximum displacement from the equilibrium level occurs at the point of release.

$v = 0$ when $x = \dfrac{l}{5}$ so amplitude $= \dfrac{l}{5}$.

So: $$v^2 = \frac{5g}{2l}\left(\frac{l^2}{25} - x^2\right)$$

v is maximum when $x = 0$.

So: $$v_{\text{max}}^2 = \frac{5g}{2l} \times \frac{l^2}{25} = \frac{gl}{10}$$

Positive square root only required as v is always positive.

The maximum speed is $\sqrt{\left(\dfrac{gl}{10}\right)}$.

Example 3

A particle P of mass 0.2 kg is attached to the mid-point of a light elastic string of natural length 0.6 m and modulus of elasticity 0.9 N. The ends of the string are attached to points L and M on a smooth horizontal table where $LM = 1$ m. The particle P is released from rest at a point A on the table between L and M where $LA = 0.7$ m.

(a) Show that P moves with simple harmonic motion.
(b) Determine the period of the motion.
(c) Find the greatest speed of P during the motion.

The point B lies between L and M, and $LB = 0.4$ m.
(d) Find the time taken by P to reach B for the first time.

Answer

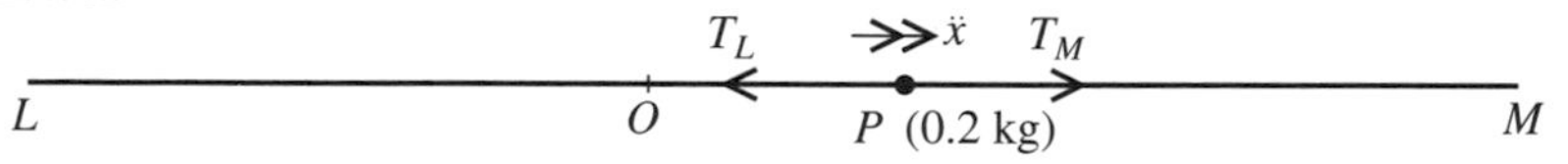

(a) The centre of the oscillation is at O, the mid-point of LM and $LO = OM = 0.5$.
Let the distance of P from O at time t seconds be x metres.
The acceleration of P is then $\ddot{x}$ in the direction OA, that is the direction of increasing x.
Because P is attached to the mid-point of the original string, consider the string to be divided into two 'half' strings, each of natural length 0.3 m. The modulus of elasticity depends only on the material the string is made from (and not the length of the string) and so will remain 0.9 N.

The extension in LP is $(0.5 + x - 0.3)$ m $= (0.2 + x)$ m.
The extension in MP is $(0.5 - x - 0.3)$ m $= (0.2 - x)$ m.

The tensions in LP and MP are found by using Hooke's law:

Hooke's law: $T = \dfrac{\lambda \times \text{ext}^n}{l}$ (chapter 2)

$$T_L = \frac{0.9(0.2+x)}{0.3} = 3(0.2+x) \qquad (1)$$

$$T_M = \frac{0.9(0.2-x)}{0.3} = 3(0.2-x) \qquad (2)$$

Using $F = ma$ for the particle P gives:

$$T_M - T_L = 0.2\ddot{x}$$

Using (1) and (2): $3(0.2-x) - 3(0.2+x) = 0.2\ddot{x}$

So: $-6x = 0.2\ddot{x}$

and: $\ddot{x} = -\frac{6}{0.2}x = -30x$

As this equation is of the form $\ddot{x} = -\omega^2 x$, P is moving with S.H.M.

(b) Period $= \dfrac{2\pi}{\omega}$

As $\ddot{x} = -30x$, $\omega^2 = 30$.

So period $= \dfrac{2\pi}{\sqrt{30}} = 1.147 = 1.15\,\text{s}$

(c) To find the greatest speed use $v^2 = \omega^2(a^2 - x^2)$ with $x = 0$.
a is the amplitude or the greatest value of x.
x is greatest when the speed of P is zero, which occurs at the point of release.
So a is $(0.7 - 0.5)\,\text{m} = 0.2\,\text{m}$.
Hence $v_{\text{max}}^2 = \omega^2 a^2 = 30 \times 0.2 = 6$.
$v_{\text{max}} = \sqrt{6} = 2.449 = 2.45\,\text{m}\,\text{s}^{-1}$.

Positive square root only required as v_{max} is positive.

(d) As P is released from an end point of the oscillation, use $x = a\cos\omega t$:

$$x = 0.2\cos\sqrt{30}t$$

Use $\sqrt{30}$ as this is exact.

As $LB = 0.4\,\text{m}$, B lies between L and O; the distance of B from O is $(0.5 - 0.4)\,\text{m} = 0.1\,\text{m}$. But B is on the opposite side of O from A, so at B $x = -0.1$.

So: $-0.1 = 0.2\cos\sqrt{30}t$

$$\cos\sqrt{30}t = \frac{-0.1}{0.2} = -0.5$$

So: $\sqrt{30}t = \arccos(-0.5) = 2.094\ldots$

$$t = 0.3823 = 0.382$$

Remember to have your calculator in radian mode.

P takes 0.382 s to reach B.

Revision exercise 3

1 A particle P, of mass 2 kg, is moving under the influence of a variable force $\mathbf{F}$. At time t seconds, the velocity $\mathbf{v}$ m s^{-1} of P is given by:

$$\mathbf{v} = 2t\mathbf{i} + e^{-t}\mathbf{j}$$

(a) Find the acceleration, $\mathbf{a}$ m s^{-2}, of P at time t seconds.
(b) Calculate, in N to two decimal places, the magnitude of $\mathbf{F}$ when $t = 0.2$. [E]

2 The Earth can be modelled as a sphere of radius R. At a distance x, $x \geqslant R$, from the centre of the earth the magnitude of the acceleration due to the Earth's gravity is A. By using the universal law of gravitation:

(a) show that $A = \dfrac{gR^2}{x^2}$.

A rocket of mass M is projected vertically into space with initial speed U from a point on the surface of the Earth.
(b) Find an expression for the speed of the rocket when it has travelled a distance X metres.
(c) State a physical factor you have ignored in your solution.

3 A particle P of mass m kg moves along the x-axis under the action of a single force directed towards the origin O. When the distance of P from O is x m, the magnitude of the force is $\dfrac{4m}{x+k}$ N, where k is a positive constant and the speed of P is v m s^{-1}. The particle is released from rest at the point A where $OA = 4k$ m.
(a) Find an expression, in terms of x and k, for v^2.
(b) Hence, or otherwise, find the work done by the force as P moves from B to O, where $OB = 3k$.

4

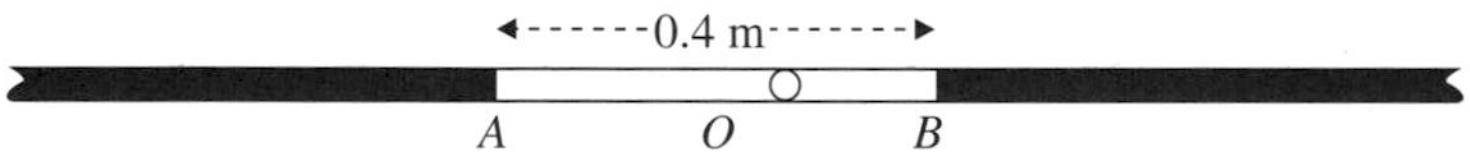

A small bubble is performing simple harmonic motion inside a long, straight narrow tube. Between points A and B, where $AB = 0.4$ m, the tube is transparent so that the bubble is visible, but elsewhere the tube is painted so that the bubble is not visible. The mid-point of AB is the point O, as shown in the diagram. The bubble attains its maximum speed at O. During its motion the bubble remains visible for intervals of 2 seconds and not visible for intervals of 4 seconds.

(a) Show that the period of the motion is 12 seconds.

(b) Find the maximum displacement of the bubble from O.

(c) Find, to two significant figures, the speed of the bubble at B. [E]

5 A particle P, of mass 0.01 kg, moves along a straight line with simple harmonic motion. The centre of the motion is the point O. At the points L and M, which are on opposite sides of O, the particle has speeds of $0.09\,\text{m s}^{-1}$ and $0.06\,\text{m s}^{-1}$ respectively and $2OL = OM = 0.02\,\text{m}$.

(a) Show that the period of this motion is $2\pi\sqrt{\left(\frac{1}{15}\right)}$ s.

Find:

(b) the greatest value of the magnitude of the force acting on P, giving your answer to two significant figures,

(c) the time for P to move directly from L through O to M, giving your answer to two significant figures. [E]

6 A particle P of mass 0.2 kg is attached to one end of a light elastic spring of modulus of elasticity 20 N and natural length 1 m. The other end of the spring is attached to the point A on a smooth horizontal floor and P is held on the floor at the point B where $AB = 1.5\,\text{m}$. P is released from rest.

(a) Show that P moves with simple harmonic motion.

Assuming that P meets no obstructions to its motion:

(b) calculate, as a multiple of π, the time that elapses before P returns to B for the first time.

7 A particle P of mass m is attached to one end of a light elastic string of natural length $4l$. The other end of the string is attached to a fixed point A. When P hangs in equilibrium at the point O the string has length $6l$.

(a) Find the modulus of elasticity of the string.

The particle is now given an impulse of magnitude I vertically downwards.

(b) Show that, while the string remains taut, P moves with simple harmonic motion.

(c) Find the time taken for P to return to O for the first time.

The particle first comes to instantaneous rest at the point B. Given that $I = 2m\sqrt{(gl)}$:

(d) find the distance OB.

Test yourself

What to review

If your answer is incorrect:

1 A particle P of mass 0.8 kg moves along the positive x-axis under the action of a single force directed towards the origin O. At time t seconds the distance of P from O is x metres, the speed of P is $v \text{ m s}^{-1}$ and the magnitude of the force is $0.4x$ N. When $t = 0$, $x = 2$ and P is moving away from O with speed 5 m s^{-1}.
(a) Find an expression for v^2 in terms of x^2.
(b) Find the distance of P from O when P comes to instantaneous rest.
(c) Find the work done by the force as P moves from the point where $x = 2$ to the point where $x = 3$.

Review Heinemann Book M3 pages 51–53 and pages 55–56

---

2 A particle P of mass 0.5 kg is moving on a horizontal plane. At time t seconds, the velocity $\mathbf{v}$ metres per second of P is given by:

$$\mathbf{v} = 4t\mathbf{i} + e^{2t}\mathbf{j},\ t \geqslant 0$$

where $\mathbf{i}$ and $\mathbf{j}$ are perpendicular vectors in the horizontal plane.
(a) Find the acceleration of P at time t seconds.
(b) Find the magnitude of the resultant force acting on P when $t = 0$. [E]

Review Heinemann Book M3 pages 51–53

---

3 A particle P describes simple harmonic motion, making three complete oscillations per second. At a certain instant, P is at the point O and is moving at its maximum speed of 5 m s^{-1}.
(a) Find the speed of P 0.05 s after it passes through O, giving your answer to three significant figures.

After passing through O, P first comes to instantaneous rest at the point A.
(b) Find the average speed of P as it moves from O to A, giving your answer to three significant figures. [E]

Review Heinemann Book M3 pages 65–70

---

4 A light elastic string of natural length 50 cm has one end A attached to a fixed point. A particle P of mass 0.2 kg is attached to the other end of the string and hangs freely in equilibrium vertically below A. The extension of the string is 10 cm.

(a) Find the modulus of elasticity of the string.

The particle is now pulled vertically downwards until the extension is 15 cm and P is released from rest.

(b) Show that P moves with simple harmonic motion.

(c) State the period and the amplitude of the motion.

(d) Find the greatest speed of P during the motion.

(e) Find the time taken by P to rise 7.5 cm.

Review Heinemann Book M3 pages 83–90

---

5 The ends of a light elastic string, of natural length l and modulus of elasticity λ, are attached to fixed points A and B on a smooth horizontal table. The distance AB is $2l$.
A particle P of mass m is attached to the mid-point of the string. The particle is released from rest at point C of the table, where A, C and B are collinear and $AC = 1.5l$.

(a) Show that P performs simple harmonic motion.

(b) Find, in terms of λ, m and l, the period of the motion.

(c) Find, in terms of λ, m and l, the maximum speed of P.

Review Heinemann Book M3 pages 75–80

Test yourself answers

1 (a) $v^2 = 27 - \frac{x^2}{2}$ **(b)** $x = \sqrt{54}$ **(c)** 1 J

2 (a) $\mathbf{a} = 4\mathbf{i} + 2e^{2t}\mathbf{j}$ **(b)** $\sqrt{5}$ N

3 (a) 2.94 m s^{-1} **(b)** 3.18 m s^{-1}

4 (a) 9.8 N **(c)** 0.635 s, 0.05 m **(d)** 0.495 m s^{-1} **(e)** 0.212 s

5 (b) $\pi\sqrt{\frac{ml}{\lambda}}$ **(c)** $\sqrt{\frac{\lambda l}{m}}$

Circular motion 4

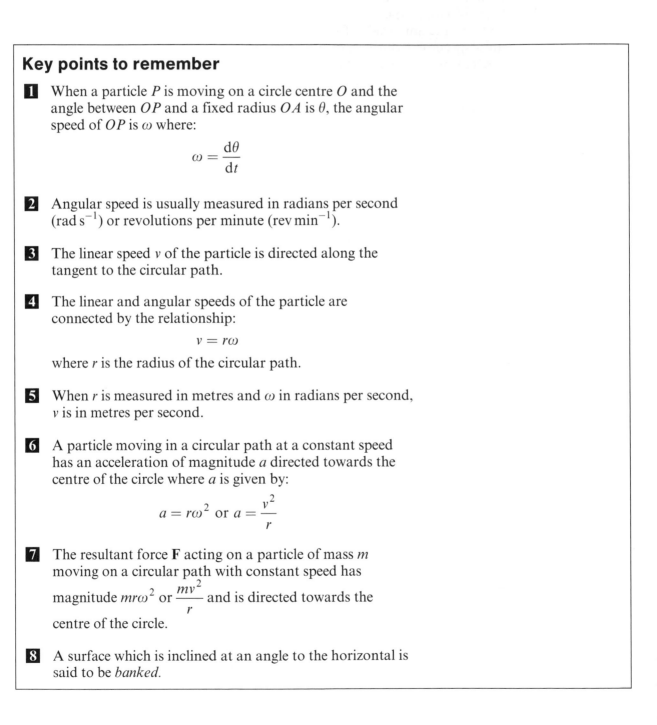

Key points to remember

1 When a particle P is moving on a circle centre O and the angle between OP and a fixed radius OA is θ, the angular speed of OP is ω where:

$$\omega = \frac{d\theta}{dt}$$

2 Angular speed is usually measured in radians per second (rad s^{-1}) or revolutions per minute (rev min^{-1}).

3 The linear speed v of the particle is directed along the tangent to the circular path.

4 The linear and angular speeds of the particle are connected by the relationship:

$$v = r\omega$$

where r is the radius of the circular path.

5 When r is measured in metres and ω in radians per second, v is in metres per second.

6 A particle moving in a circular path at a constant speed has an acceleration of magnitude a directed towards the centre of the circle where a is given by:

$$a = r\omega^2 \text{ or } a = \frac{v^2}{r}$$

7 The resultant force **F** acting on a particle of mass m moving on a circular path with constant speed has magnitude $mr\omega^2$ or $\frac{mv^2}{r}$ and is directed towards the centre of the circle.

8 A surface which is inclined at an angle to the horizontal is said to be *banked*.

Motion of a particle in a vertical circle

9 A particle which is moving in a *vertical* circle has variable speed.

10 The acceleration of a particle moving in a circle of radius r with speed v at time t has two components:

$\frac{v^2}{r}$ towards the centre of the circle

and $\frac{\mathrm{d}v}{\mathrm{d}t}$ along the tangent

11 The component of the force along the radius does no work during the motion.

12 By the work–energy principle, the sum of the kinetic energy (K.E.) and gravitational potential energy (G.P.E.) of the particle is constant throughout the motion.

13 A particle which cannot leave its vertical circular path (for example a particle attached to the end of a rod) will describe complete circles provided its speed at the highest point of the circle is greater than or equal to zero.

14 A particle which can leave its vertical path (for example a particle attached to the end of a string) will do so when the force towards the centre of the circle is zero.

Example 1

A light straight rod PQR rests on a smooth horizontal table and rotates at $6\,\text{rad s}^{-1}$ about a pivot at Q. Particles of mass 2 kg and 5 kg are attached to the rod at P and R respectively.
Given that $PQ = 0.75$ m and that the horizontal force acting on the pivot at Q due to the particle at P has half the magnitude of that due to the particle at R, calculate:
(a) the length of QR
(b) the speed of the particle attached to the rod at P.

Answer

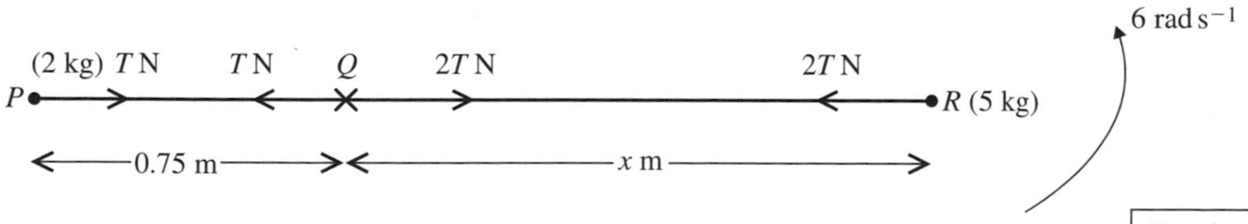

Tension in $QR = 2 \times$ tension in PQ.

(a) Let the length of PQ be x m and the tension in PQ be T N. Using **7**, the force towards Q acting on a particle of mass m is $mr\omega^2$. So the equation of motion for the particle at P (2 kg) is:

$$T = 2 \times 0.75 \times 36 = 54$$

and the equation of motion for the particle at R (5 kg) is:

$$2T = 5 \times 36x \Rightarrow T = 5 \times 18x = 90x$$

So:

$$90x = 54$$

$$x = \frac{54}{90} = 0.6$$

QR has length 0.6 m.

(b) Using **4**: $v = r\omega$.

So: $$v_P = 0.75 \times 6 = 4.5$$

The speed of the particle at P is $4.5\,\text{m}\,\text{s}^{-1}$.

Worked examination question 1 [E]

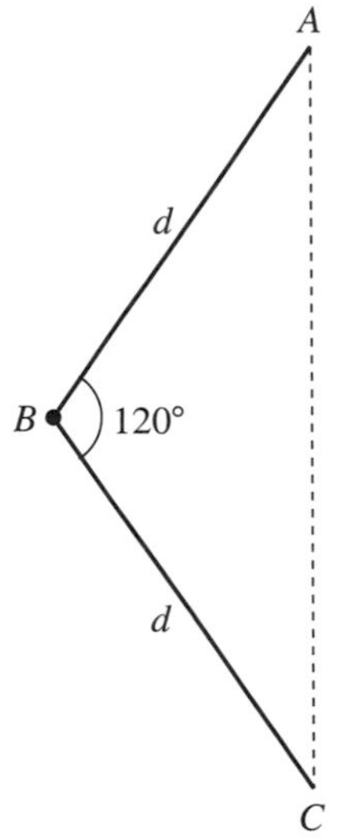

The diagram shows two light inextensible strings AB and BC, each of length d, attached at B to a particle of mass m. The other ends A and C are fixed to points in a vertical line with A above C. With both strings taut and $\angle ABC = 120°$, the particle moves in a horizontal circle with constant angular speed ω.
Find, in terms of m, g, d and ω:

(a) the tension in string AB

(b) the tension in string BC.

(c) Show that:

$$\omega^2 \geqslant \left(\frac{2g}{3d}\right)\sqrt{3}$$

Answer

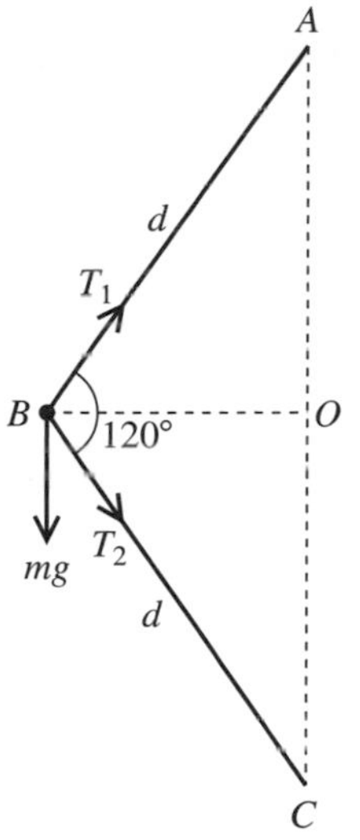

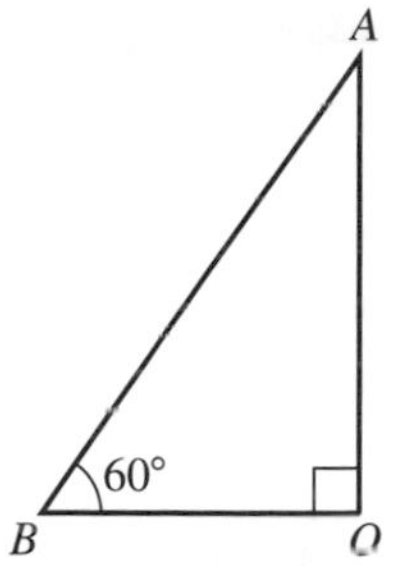

(a) Using **6**, the force towards the centre O of the circular path is $mr\omega^2$.
As $r = d\cos 60° = \frac{1}{2}d$, the force is $\frac{1}{2}md\omega^2$.

So resolving $\rightarrow$: $\frac{1}{2}md\omega^2 - T_1\cos 60° - T_2\cos 60° = 0$

or: $$\frac{1}{2}md\omega^2 = \frac{1}{2}T_1 + \frac{1}{2}T_2$$

so: $$md\omega^2 = T_1 + T_2 \qquad (1)$$

Resolving $\uparrow$: $T_1\cos 30° - T_2\cos 30° - mg = 0$

or: $$T_1 \times \frac{\sqrt{3}}{2} = T_2 \times \frac{\sqrt{3}}{2} + mg$$

so: $$T_1\sqrt{3} = T_2 \times \sqrt{3} + 2mg \qquad (2)$$

From (1): $$T_2 = md\omega^2 - T_1$$

Substituting in (2): $$T_1\sqrt{3} = (md\omega^2 - T_1)\sqrt{3} + 2mg$$

so: $$2T_1\sqrt{3} = md\omega^2\sqrt{3} + 2mg$$

$$T_1 = \frac{1}{2}md\omega^2 + \frac{1}{\sqrt{3}}mg \qquad (3)$$

(b) From (1): $T_2 = md\omega^2 - T_1$

So, using (3): $$T_2 = md\omega^2 - \frac{1}{2}md\omega^2 - \frac{1}{\sqrt{3}}mg$$

$$= \frac{1}{2}md\omega^2 - \frac{1}{\sqrt{3}}mg$$

(c) Both strings are taut, but $T_1 = \frac{1}{2}md\omega^2 + \frac{1}{\sqrt{3}}mg$ and so $T_1 > 0$ whatever the value of ω.
So we must ensure that $T_2 \geqslant 0$.

$$\tfrac{1}{2}md\omega^2 - \frac{1}{\sqrt{3}}mg \geqslant 0$$

$$\tfrac{1}{2}d\omega^2 \geqslant \frac{1}{\sqrt{3}}g$$

$$\omega^2 \geqslant \frac{2g}{\sqrt{3}d} = \left(\frac{2g}{3d}\right)\sqrt{3}$$

Example 2

A van of mass 2000 kg is rounding a bend on a road that is banked at 12° to the horizontal. The coefficient of friction between the van's tyres and the road is 0.2. The van is modelled as a particle moving at constant speed in a horizontal circle of radius 400 m. Calculate the maximum speed at which the van can travel if no slipping is to occur.

Answer

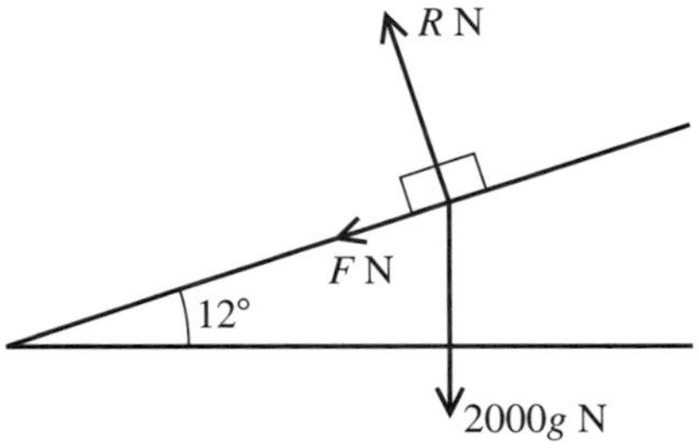

Let the maximum speed of the van be $v\,\mathrm{m\,s^{-1}}$.

Using **7**, the force towards the centre of the circle is $\left(\frac{2000v^2}{400}\right)\mathrm{N} = (5v^2)\,\mathrm{N}$.

The equation of motion towards the centre of the circle gives:

$$R\sin 12° + F\cos 12° = 5v^2 \qquad (1)$$

There is no vertical motion.

Resolving ↑: $R\cos 12° - F\sin 12° - 2000g = 0$ (2)

At maximum speed friction is limiting.

Using $F = \mu R$ gives $F = 0.2R$.
Substituting for F in (1):

$$R\sin 12° + 0.2R\cos 12° = 5v^2$$

$$R(\sin 12° + 0.2\cos 12°) = 5v^2 \qquad (3)$$

and in (2):

$$R\cos 12° = 0.2R\sin 12° + 2000g$$

$$R(\cos 12° - 0.2\sin 12°) = 2000g \qquad (4)$$

Dividing equation (3) by equation (4):

$$\frac{\sin 12^\circ + 0.2\cos 12^\circ}{\cos 12^\circ - 0.2\sin 12^\circ} = \frac{5v^2}{2000g}$$

$$v^2 = 400g\left(\frac{\sin 12^\circ + 0.2\cos 12^\circ}{\cos 12^\circ - 0.2\sin 12^\circ}\right)$$

$$v = 41.09$$

The maximum speed is $41.1\,\text{m s}^{-1}$.

Worked examination question 2 [E]

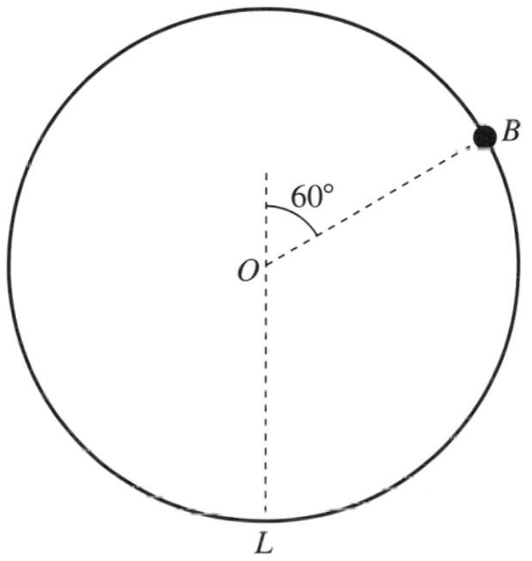

A small bead B, of mass m, is threaded onto a smooth circular wire with centre O and radius r. The wire is fixed in a vertical plane and initially B is at the position where OB makes an angle of 60° with the upward vertical, as shown in the diagram. The lowest point of the wire is L. The bead is released from rest. Find:

(a) the speed of B as it passes through L

(b) the magnitude of the force exerted by the wire on B when it passes through L.

Answer

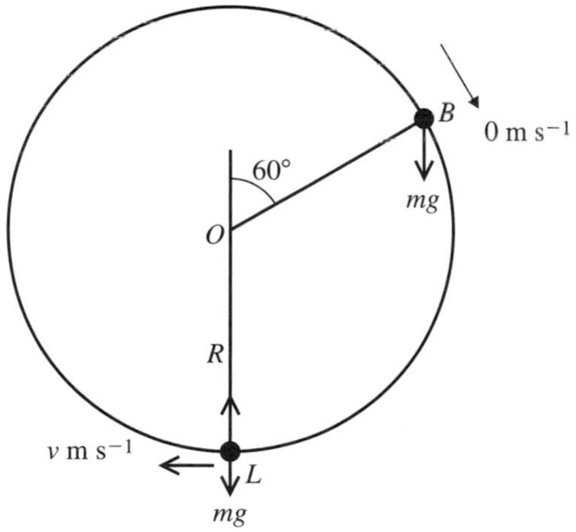

(a) Consider the motion of B from release to L:

initial K.E. $= 0$

final K.E. $= \frac{1}{2}mv^2$ where v is the speed of B at L

G.P.E. lost $= mgr(1 + \cos 60°) = mgr\left(1 + \frac{1}{2}\right) = \frac{3}{2}mgr$

Using **12**:

$$\frac{1}{2}mv^2 = \frac{3}{2}mgr$$
$$v^2 = 3gr$$
$$v = \sqrt{(3gr)}$$

(b) Using **10**, the acceleration along the radius at L is $\dfrac{v^2}{r}$. The equation of motion along the radius at L is:

$$R - mg = m\frac{v^2}{r}$$

So:

$$R - mg = 3mg$$
$$R = 4mg$$

From **(a)**: $v^2 = 3rg$

Worked examination question 3 [E]

One end of a light inextensible string of length 0.25 m is tied to a fixed point A. A particle P, of mass 0.15 kg, is tied at the other end of the string and hangs freely in equilibrium. The particle P is projected horizontally with speed $4\,\text{m}\,\text{s}^{-1}$ so that P moves in a complete vertical circle, centre A. Giving your answers to two significant figures, calculate:

(a) the least speed of P

(b) the tension in the string at the instant when the speed of P is least.

Answer

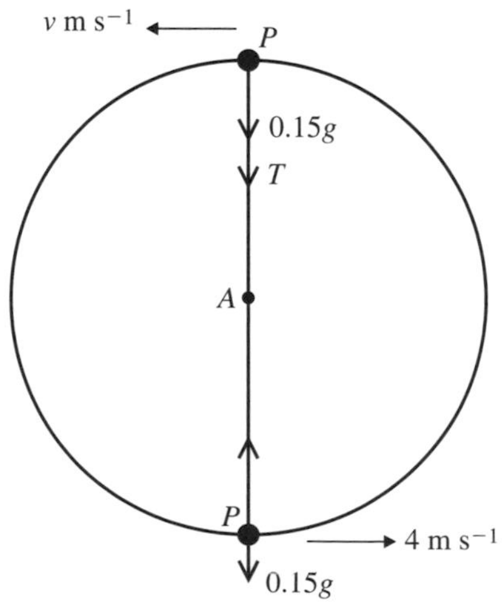

(a) Let the least speed of the particle be $v\,\text{m s}^{-1}$.
Consider the motion from the bottom to the top of the circle:

> Least speed occurs when maximum G.P.E. has been gained, that is at the top.

$$\text{initial K.E.} = \tfrac{1}{2}mV^2 = \tfrac{1}{2} \times 0.15 \times 16$$

$$\text{final K.E.} = \tfrac{1}{2}mv^2$$

$$\text{G.P.E. gained} = mgh = 0.15 \times 2 \times 0.25g$$

Using **12**:

$$\text{K.E. lost} = \text{G.P.E. gained}$$

So: $$\tfrac{1}{2} \times 0.15 \times 16 - \tfrac{1}{2} \times 0.15v^2 = 0.15 \times 2 \times 0.25g$$

$$16 - v^2 = g$$

$$v^2 = 16 - g$$

$$v = 2.48$$

The minimum speed is $2.5\,\text{m s}^{-1}$.

> The answer was required to two significant figures.

(c) Using **10**, the acceleration along the radius at the top is $\dfrac{v^2}{0.25} = \dfrac{16-g}{0.25} = \dfrac{6.2}{0.25}$. Using the equation of motion along the radius at the top gives:

> Use the accurate value for v^2, not the rounded answer.

$$mg + T = 0.15 \times \frac{6.2}{0.25}$$

$$0.15 \times 9.8 + T = 0.15 \times \frac{6.2}{0.25}$$

$$T = 0.15 \times \frac{6.2}{0.25} - 0.15 \times 9.8$$

$$T = 2.25$$

The tension is 2.3 N.

Example 3

A smooth hemisphere of radius a is fixed with its plane surface on a horizontal floor. A small stone is initially at rest at the highest point A of the hemisphere. The stone is disturbed and begins to slide on the surface of the hemisphere. By modelling the stone as a particle with initial speed zero, find, in terms of a, the height of P above the floor at the instant when P leaves the surface of the hemisphere.

Answer

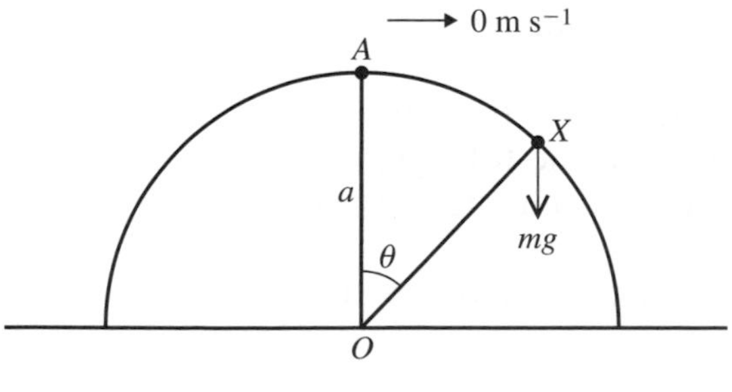

Let the stone leave the sphere at X and let $\angle AOX = \theta$. Consider the motion from A to X.

initial K.E. $= 0$

final K.E. $= \frac{1}{2}mv^2$, where v is the speed of the stone at X

G.P.E. lost $= mgh = mga(1 - \cos\theta)$

Using **12**:

$$\tfrac{1}{2}mv^2 = mga(1 - \cos\theta)$$
$$mv^2 = 2mga(1 - \cos\theta)$$

At X the reaction between the particle and the hemisphere is zero.

Using **14**

Using **7**, the force towards the centre is $\dfrac{mv^2}{a}$.

The equation of motion along the radius at X gives:

$$mg\cos\theta = \frac{mv^2}{a}$$
$$mg\cos\theta = \frac{2mga(1 - \cos\theta)}{a}$$
$$\cos\theta = 2(1 - \cos\theta)$$
$$3\cos\theta = 2$$
$$\cos\theta = \tfrac{2}{3}$$

Height above the floor $= a\cos\theta = \frac{2}{3}a$.

Worked examination question 4 [E]

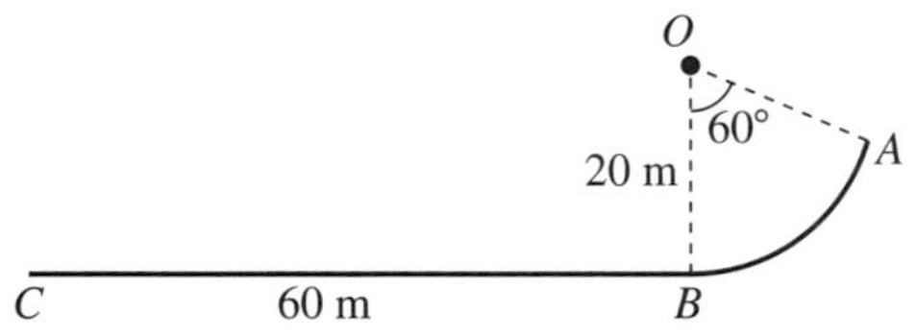

A toboggan of mass 10 kg starts from rest at point A and descends a smooth slope in the shape of an arc AB of a circle radius 20 m and centre O. The points A and B are such that OB is vertical and $\angle AOB = 60°$.

After passing through B, the toboggan continues along a rough horizontal plane, coming to rest at point C, where $BC = 60$ m. Points O, A, B and C are in the same vertical plane, as shown in the diagram.

(a) Find the speed of the toboggan at B.

(b) Show that, at the point B, the magnitude of the normal component of the force exerted by the ground on the toboggan is instantaneously halved, as the toboggan moves from the curved slope to the level plane.

(c) Calculate the value of the coefficient of friction between the toboggan and the horizontal plane.

Answer

(a) Consider the motion of the toboggan from A to B:

G.P.E. lost $= mgh = 10g \times 20(1 - \cos 60°) = 10g \times 20\left(1 - \frac{1}{2}\right) = 100g$

Let the speed of the toboggan at B be v:

initial K.E. $= 0$ at A

final K.E. $= \frac{1}{2}mv^2 = \frac{1}{2} \times 10v^2 = 5v^2$ at B

Using **12**:

$$5v^2 = 100g$$
$$v^2 = 20g = 196$$
$$v = 14$$

The speed at B is $14\,\text{m}\,\text{s}^{-1}$.

(b) At B, the acceleration towards O is $\frac{v^2}{r} = \frac{196}{20}$.

Using **10**

The equation of motion along the radius BO gives:

$$R_1 - 10g = 10 \times \tfrac{196}{20}$$
$$R_1 = \tfrac{196}{20} + 98 = 196$$

where R_1 is the normal reaction.
When the toboggan is moving on the horizontal part BC:
Resolving ↑:

$$R_2 = 10g = 98$$

where R_2 is the normal reaction.
Thus the magnitude of the normal reaction has halved as B moves from the curved slope to the level plane.

The only acceleration is now horizontal.

(c) Let the frictional force be F.
Work done against friction as the toboggan moves from B to $C = 60 \times F$. K.E. lost as the toboggan moves from B to $C = 980\,\text{J}$ as it comes to rest at C.
By the work–energy principle:

$$60 \times F = 980$$

So: $$F = \tfrac{980}{60}$$

Using $\frac{F}{R_2} = \mu$ gives $\mu = \frac{980}{60} \div 98 = \frac{1}{6}$.

From **(b)** $R_2 = 98$

Revision exercise 4

1 A particle of mass 0.1 kg rests on the smooth surface of a horizontal disc of radius 0.6 m. The particle is attached to the ends of two light rods, each of length 0.8 m, and the other ends of the rods are fastened to the disc at opposite ends of a diameter. The disc is made to rotate about a vertical axis through its centre at $10\,\text{rad}\,\text{s}^{-1}$.

(a) Calculate the tension in each of the rods.

The rods will break if subjected to a tension greater than 25 N.

(b) Find the maximum speed at which the disc can rotate without the rods breaking. [E]

2 Two light strings, AB and BC, are each attached at B to a particle of mass m. The string AB is elastic, of natural length $2a$ and modulus $3mg$. The string BC is inextensible and of length $3a$. The ends A and C are fixed with C vertically below A and $AC = 5a$.

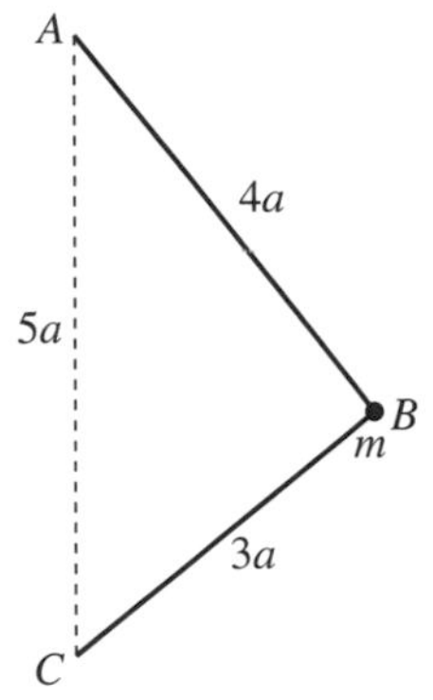

The particle moves with constant speed in a horizontal circle, with both strings taut and $AB = 4a$, as shown in the diagram.

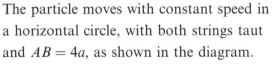

(a) Find the tension in the string AB.

(b) Find the tension in the string BC.

(c) Show that the speed of the particle is $\sqrt{\left(\frac{44}{5}ga\right)}$. [E]

3

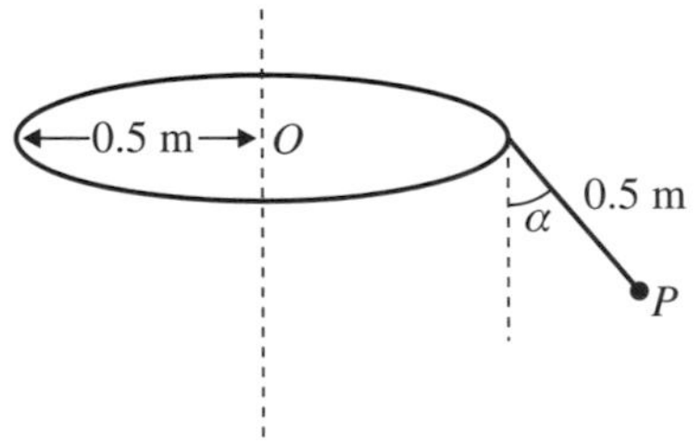

A light inextensible string of length 0.5 m is attached to a point on the circumference of a disc of radius 0.5 m. To the other end of the string is attached a small stone P of mass M kg. The disc is made to rotate in a horizontal plane about a vertical axis through its centre O. At each instant the string lies in a vertical plane through O. Given that the disc rotates at a constant rate of 2 rad s^{-1}, and that the string makes a constant angle α with the downwards vertical, as shown in the diagram, show that:

$$\cot\alpha + \cos\alpha = 4.9$$ [E]

4 A particle of mass 2 kg is attached to one end of a light inextensible cord, the other end of which is fixed at a point O. The particle moves with speed $5\,\text{m}\,\text{s}^{-1}$ in a horizontal circle of radius 6 m and whose centre is vertically below O. Calculate:

(a) the magnitude of the tension in the cord

(b) the length of the cord.

The path of the particle is at a height of 20 m above level ground when the cord breaks.

(c) Find the tangent of the angle that the velocity of the particle makes with the horizontal when the particle strikes the ground. [E]

5 A particle P, of mass M, moves on the smooth inner surface of a fixed hollow spherical bowl, centre O and inner radius r, describing a horizontal circle at a constant speed. The centre C of this circle is at a depth $\frac{1}{3}r$ vertically below O. Determine:

(a) the magnitude of the force exerted by the surface of the sphere on P

(b) the speed of P. [E]

6 A particle P, of mass m, is attached to a fixed point O by a light inextensible string of length a, and is executing complete circular revolutions in a vertical plane. Show that when OP is inclined at an angle θ to the downward vertical, the tension T in the string is given by:

$$T = mg(3\cos\theta - 2) + \frac{mu^2}{a}$$

where u is the speed of P when it passes through its lowest point. Deduce that $u^2 \geqslant 5ga$.

Show also that, if $3T_0$ and T_0 are the greatest and least tensions in the string during the motion, then:

$$u^2 = 8ag \text{ and } T = T_0(2 + \cos\theta)$$ [E]

7 A particle P of mass m lies inside a fixed smooth hollow sphere of internal radius a and centre O. When P is at rest at the lowest point A of the sphere, it is given a horizontal impulse of magnitude mu.

The particle P loses contact with the inner surface of the sphere at point B, where $\angle AOB = 120°$.

(a) Show that $u^2 = \frac{7}{2}ga$.

(b) Find the greatest height above B reached by P. [E]

8

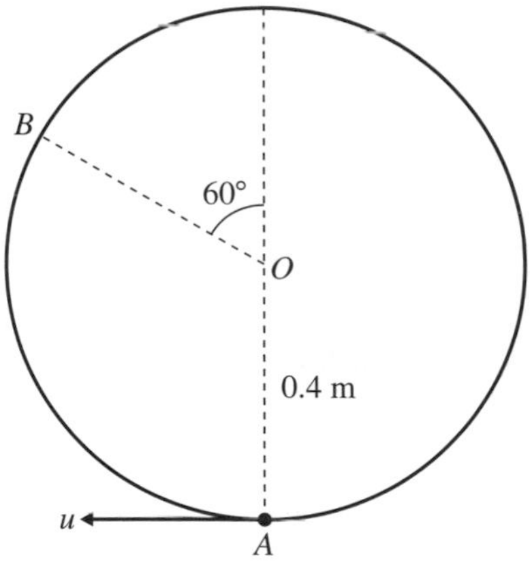

A particle P moves inside a smooth hollow cylinder of internal radius 0.4 m, fixed with its axis horizontal. The point O is on the axis of the cylinder.
The particle is projected with speed u metres per second, horizontally and perpendicular to the axis of the cylinder, from point A, which is on the inner surface of the cylinder vertically below O. At point B, where OB makes an angle of 60° with the vertical, as shown in the diagram, P loses contact with the inner surface of the cylinder.

(a) Show that the speed of P at B is $1.4\,\text{m s}^{-1}$.

(b) Find the value of u, giving your answer to one decimal place.

(c) Find the greatest height above O reached by P. [E]

Test yourself

What to review

If your answer is incorrect:

1 A particle P, of mass 0.2 kg, is attached to one end of a light inextensible string of length 1.2 m. The other end of the string is fixed to a point O. The particle P moves with uniform speed in a horizontal circle whose centre is directly below O. The time taken by P to complete one circular orbit is 1.4 s. Find:
(a) the acute angle between OP and the vertical, giving your answer to the nearest degree
(b) the tension in the string, giving your answer to the nearest 0.1 N. [E]

Review Heinemann Book M3 pages 126–130

2 A car is travelling round a bend in a road that is banked at an angle of 25° to the horizontal. The coefficient of friction between the car's tyres and the road surface is 0.4. The car can be modelled as a particle moving in a horizontal circle of radius 90 m. The car rounds the bend without slipping. Find:
(a) the greatest speed at which the car can travel
(b) the least speed at which the car can travel.

Review Heinemann Book M3 pages 131–134

3

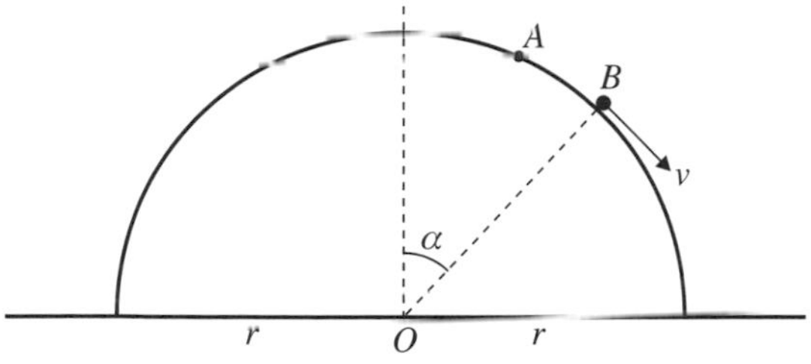

The diagram shows a smooth solid hemisphere H of radius r fixed with its plane surface, centre O, in contact with horizontal ground. A particle is released from rest on the surface of H at a point A such that OA makes an angle $\arccos \frac{7}{8}$ with the upward vertical. The particle slides freely until it leaves the surface of H at the point B with speed v. Given that OB makes an angle α with the upward vertical:
(a) show that $\cos \alpha = \frac{7}{12}$
(b) find v^2 in terms of g and r.

Given that the particle strikes the ground with speed U,
(c) find U^2 in terms of g and r. [E]

Review Heinemann Book M3 pages 145–155

---

4 A light inextensible string OA of length a has one end O attached to a fixed point and hangs vertically at rest with a particle of mass m attached to the other end A. The particle is projected horizontally with speed $\sqrt{(nga)}$.
Assuming that the string remains taut, show that when it has turned through an angle θ the tension in the string is:

$$mg(n - 2 + 3\cos\theta)$$

(a) Determine the value of n given that the string just becomes slack when the particle is at a height $\frac{1}{2}a$ above O.
(b) Find the condition satisfied by n when the particle describes complete circles about O.
(c) Describe the motion of the particle when $n \leqslant 2$. [E]

Review Heinemann Book M3 pages 145–155

Test yourself answers

1 (a) 66° **(b)** 4.8 N
2 (a) $30.6\,\text{m s}^{-1}$ **(b)** $7.02\,\text{m s}^{-1}$
3 (b) $\frac{7rg}{12}$ **(c)** $\frac{7rg}{4}$
4 (a) $n = \frac{7}{2}$ **(b)** $n \geqslant 5$ **(c)** pendulum, max. deflection $\pm \arccos\left(\frac{2-n}{2}\right)$

Statics of rigid bodies 5

Key points to remember

1

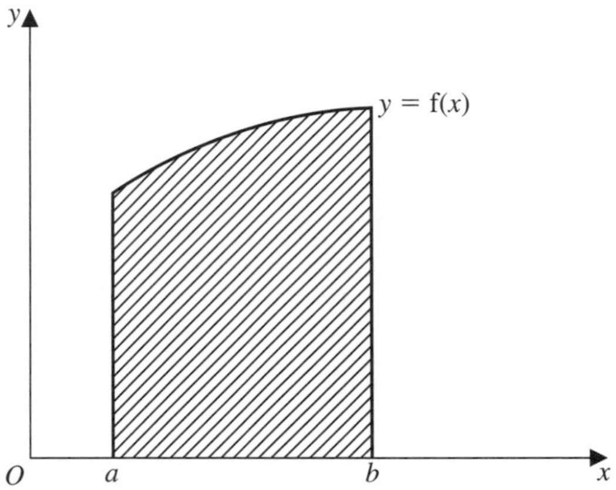

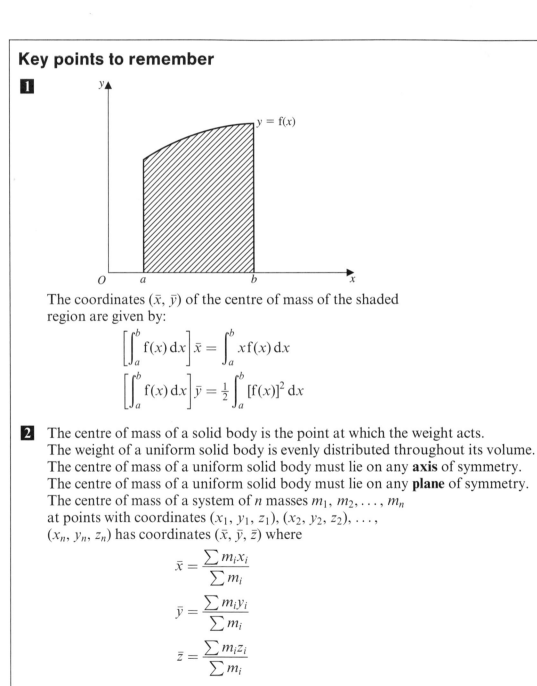

The coordinates $(\bar{x}, \bar{y})$ of the centre of mass of the shaded region are given by:

$$\left[\int_a^b f(x)\,dx\right]\bar{x} = \int_a^b x f(x)\,dx$$

$$\left[\int_a^b f(x)\,dx\right]\bar{y} = \frac{1}{2}\int_a^b [f(x)]^2\,dx$$

2 The centre of mass of a solid body is the point at which the weight acts.
The weight of a uniform solid body is evenly distributed throughout its volume.
The centre of mass of a uniform solid body must lie on any **axis** of symmetry.
The centre of mass of a uniform solid body must lie on any **plane** of symmetry.
The centre of mass of a system of n masses $m_1, m_2, \ldots, m_n$ at points with coordinates $(x_1, y_1, z_1), (x_2, y_2, z_2), \ldots, (x_n, y_n, z_n)$ has coordinates $(\bar{x}, \bar{y}, \bar{z})$ where

$$\bar{x} = \frac{\sum m_i x_i}{\sum m_i}$$

$$\bar{y} = \frac{\sum m_i y_i}{\sum m_i}$$

$$\bar{z} = \frac{\sum m_i z_i}{\sum m_i}$$

3

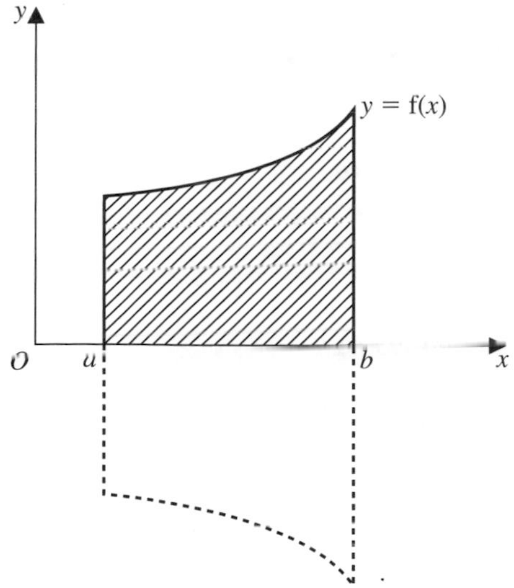

The x-coordinate of the centre of mass, $\bar{x}$, of the solid of revolution generated when the shaded region is rotated through 360° about the x-axis is given by:

$$M\bar{x} = \left[\int_a^b \rho\pi y^2 \, dx\right]\bar{x} = \int_a^b \rho\pi y^2 x \, dx$$

4 **Standard results for uniform bodies**

Body	Centre of mass
Solid hemisphere, radius r	$\frac{3}{8}r$ from centre
Hemispherical shell, radius r	$\frac{1}{2}r$ from centre
Circular arc, radius r, angle at centre 2α	$\frac{r \sin \alpha}{\alpha}$ from centre
Sector of circle, radius r, angle at centre 2α	$\frac{2r \sin \alpha}{3\alpha}$ from centre
Solid right circular cone, height h	$\frac{3h}{4}$ from vertex
Conical shell, height h	$\frac{2h}{3}$ from vertex

5 A rigid body is in **equilibrium** if:

(i) the vector sum of the forces acting is zero, that is the sum of the components of the forces in any given direction is zero

(ii) the algebraic sum of the moments of the forces about any given point is zero.

6 A rigid body hangs in equilibrium with its centre of mass vertically below the point of suspension.
For a body in contact with a horizontal or inclined plane to be in equilibrium, the line of action of the weight, through the centre of mass, must lie inside the area of contact.

7 To decide if equilibrium will be broken by sliding or toppling two cases need to be examined:
(i) when the body is on the point of sliding so that $F = \mu R$
(ii) when the body is on the point of toppling, so that the reaction acts at the point about which the body will turn.

Worked examination question 1 [E]

Find the coordinates of the centre of mass of a uniform lamina bounded by the curve $y^2 = x^3$, where $y > 0$, the x-axis and the line $x = 4$. This lamina is suspended freely from the origin O. Find, to the nearest degree, the inclination to the vertical of the x-axis.

[E]

Answer

The lamina under consideration is shown shaded in the diagram. The equation of the bounding curve is $y = x^{3/2}$ so the area of the lamina is:

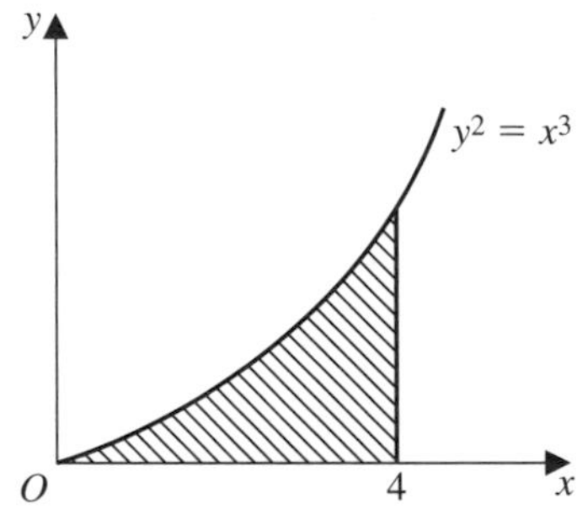

$$A = \int y\,dx = \int_0^4 x^{3/2}\,dx$$

Integrating:

$$A = \left[\frac{x^{\frac{5}{2}}}{5/2}\right]_0^4 = \tfrac{2}{5}(4)^{\frac{5}{2}} = \tfrac{64}{5}$$

The x-coordinate of the centre of mass G is given by:

$$A\bar{x} = \int_0^4 x\,x^{3/2}\,dx$$ Using **1**

$$= \int_0^4 x^{5/2}\,dx$$

$$= \left[\frac{x^{7/2}}{7/2}\right]_0^4$$

$$= \tfrac{2}{7}(4)^{\frac{7}{2}}$$

$$= \tfrac{256}{7}$$

So: $$\bar{x} = \tfrac{256}{7} \times \tfrac{5}{64} = \tfrac{20}{7} = 2\tfrac{6}{7}$$

The y-coordinate of the centre of mass G is given by:

$$A\bar{y} = \frac{1}{2}\int_0^4 [x^{3/2}]^2\,dx$$

Using 1

$$= \frac{1}{2}\int_0^4 x^3\,dx$$

$$= \frac{1}{2}\left[\frac{x^4}{4}\right]_0^4$$

$$= \frac{1}{8} \times 256$$

$$= 32$$

So: $\bar{y} = 32 \times \frac{5}{64} = \frac{5}{2} = 2\frac{1}{2}$

When the lamina is suspended from O the situation is:

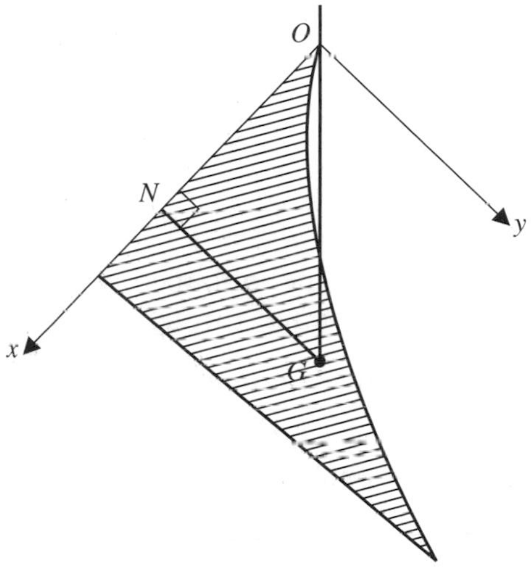

$$ON = \bar{x} = 2\tfrac{6}{7}$$

$$NG = \bar{y} = 2\tfrac{1}{2}$$

If $\angle NOG = \theta$, then $\tan\theta = \dfrac{NG}{ON}$

so: $\tan\theta = \frac{5}{2} \times \frac{7}{20} = \frac{7}{8}$

$\theta = \arctan\left(\frac{7}{8}\right) = 41.2° = 41°$ (to the nearest degree)

Worked examination question 2 [E]

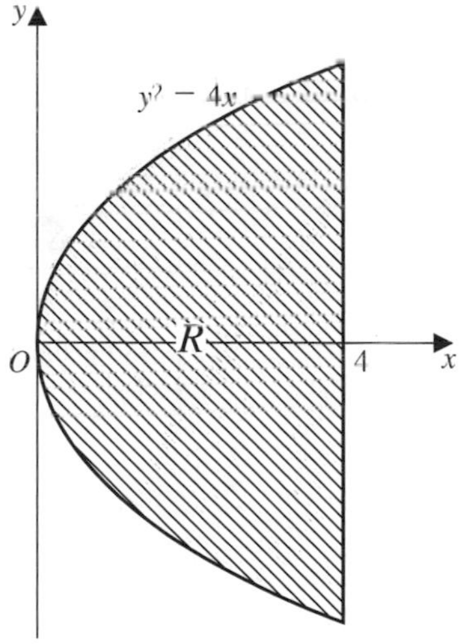

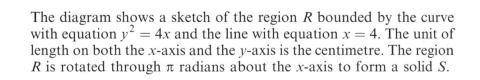

The diagram shows a sketch of the region R bounded by the curve with equation $y^2 = 4x$ and the line with equation $x = 4$. The unit of length on both the x-axis and the y-axis is the centimetre. The region R is rotated through π radians about the x-axis to form a solid S.

(a) Show that the volume of S is $32\pi\,\text{cm}^3$.

Given that the solid S is uniform:
(b) find the distance of the centre of mass of S from O.

Answer

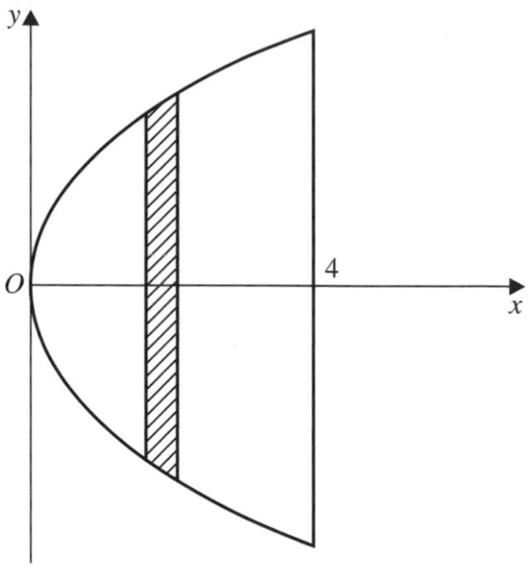

(a) The volume obtained when the shaded strip in the above diagram is rotated through π radians about Ox is $\delta V = \pi y^2 \delta x$

So the required volume $V = \int_0^4 \pi y^2\,dx$

Using the equation of the curve:

$$V = \pi \int_0^4 4x\,dx$$
$$= 4\pi \left[\frac{x^2}{2}\right]_0^4 = 4\pi\,\tfrac{16}{2}$$
$$= 32\pi\,\text{cm}^3$$

(b) The centre of mass will lie on Ox, the axis of symmetry of S. The x-coordinate of the centre of mass, $\bar{x}$, is given by:

$$V\bar{x} = \int_0^4 x(\pi y^2\,dx)$$

Using **3**

$$= \pi \int_0^4 x\,4x\,dx$$

Using the equation of the curve.

$$= 4\pi \int_0^4 x^2\,dx$$
$$= 4\pi \left[\frac{x^3}{3}\right]_0^4$$
$$= 4\pi\,\tfrac{64}{3}$$
$$= \frac{256\pi}{3}$$

So: $$\bar{x} = \frac{256\pi}{3} \times \frac{1}{32\pi} = \tfrac{8}{3}\,\text{cm}$$

Worked examination question 3 [E]

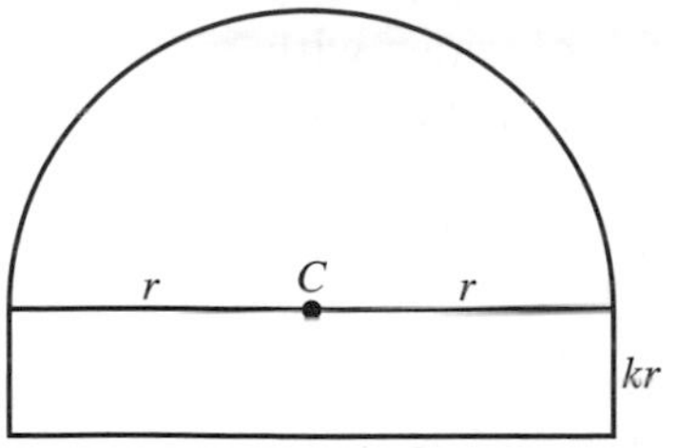

The diagram shows a cross-section containing the axis of symmetry of a uniform body consisting of a solid right circular cylinder of base radius r and height kr surmounted by a solid hemisphere of radius r. Given that the centre of mass of the body is at the centre C of the common face of the cylinder and the hemisphere, find the value of k, giving your answer to two significant figures.
Explain briefly why the body remains at rest when it is placed with any point of its hemispherical surface in contact with a horizontal plane. [E]

Answer

The mass of the hemisphere is:

$$\tfrac{1}{2}\left(\tfrac{4}{3}\pi r^3\right)\rho = \tfrac{2}{3}\pi r^3 \rho$$

Using the result in the formula book, the centre of mass of the hemisphere is $\frac{3}{8}r$ from C along the axis of symmetry.
The mass of the cylinder is:

$$\pi r^2 kr\rho = k\pi r^3 \rho$$

The centre of mass of the cylinder is at the mid-point of the axis of symmetry, that is $\frac{1}{2}kr$ from C.

In the above we have taken ρ to be the common density of the cylinder and the hemisphere.
As the centre of mass is at C:

$$\left(\tfrac{2}{3}\pi r^3 \rho\right) \times \tfrac{3}{8}r = (k\pi r^3 \rho) \times \frac{kr}{2}$$

or: $$\tfrac{1}{4} = \frac{k^2}{2}$$

So: $$k^2 = \tfrac{1}{2}$$

$$k = \frac{1}{\sqrt{2}}$$

$$= 0.71$$

When the body is placed with any point of the hemispherical surface in contact with the horizontal plane its centre of mass is C and this will always be vertically above the point of contact A (see diagram) therefore there will be no turning moment.

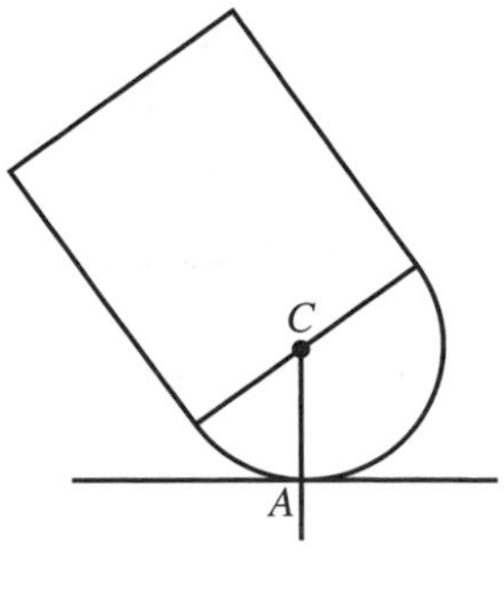

Example 1

From a uniform right circular cylinder, of radius r and height h, a right circular cone is removed. The base of the cone coincides with one end of the cylinder and its vertex O is at the centre of the other end, as shown in the diagram.

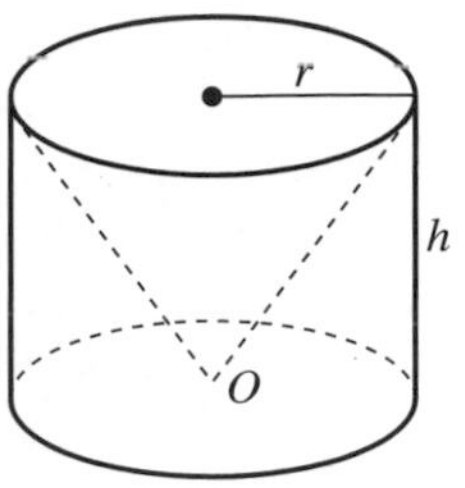

(a) Show that the centre of gravity of the remaining solid S is at a distance $\frac{3h}{8}$ from O.

The solid S is placed on a rough plane with O uppermost. The plane is inclined at an angle α to the horizontal. Given that the plane is sufficiently rough to prevent sliding:

(b) show that the solid will topple over if $\tan\alpha > \frac{8r}{5h}$.

Answer

(a) Cylinder: mass $= \pi r^2 h\rho$

Centre of mass distance $\frac{h}{2}$ from O on its axis of symmetry.

Cone: mass $= \frac{1}{3}\pi r^2 h\rho$

Centre of mass distance $\frac{3h}{4}$ from O on its axis of symmetry.

See formula book.

Solid S: mass $= \pi r^2 h\rho - \frac{1}{3}\pi r^2 h\rho$

$= \frac{2}{3}\pi r^2 h\rho$

Centre of mass distance d from O on its axis of symmetry.

Using the above information and cylinder = cone + solid S:

$$(\pi r^2 h\rho) \times \frac{h}{2} = \left(\tfrac{1}{3}\pi r^2 h\rho\right) \times \frac{3h}{4} + \left(\tfrac{2}{3}\pi r^2 h\rho\right) \times d$$

So:

$$\tfrac{1}{2}h = \tfrac{1}{4}h + \tfrac{2}{3}d$$

$$d = \tfrac{3}{2}\left(\tfrac{1}{2} - \tfrac{1}{4}\right)h$$

$$= \tfrac{3}{8}h$$

(b)

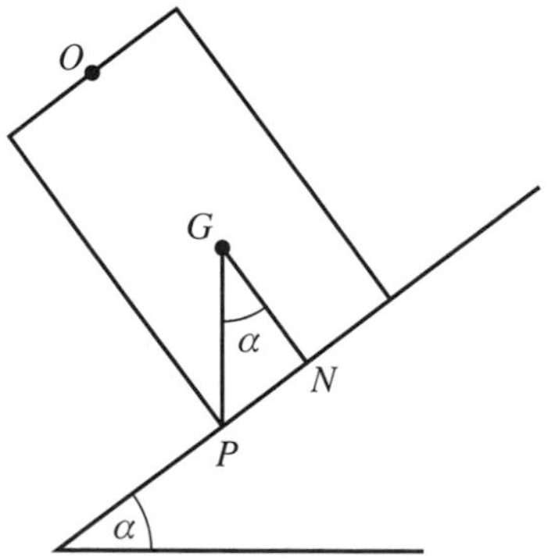

$$GN = ON - OG$$

$$= h - \tfrac{3}{8}h = \frac{5h}{8}$$

$$PN = r$$

The limiting case is shown in the diagram.

Here $\tan\alpha = \dfrac{PN}{GN} = r \bigg/ \left(\dfrac{5h}{8}\right)$

$$= \frac{8r}{5h}$$

So solid will topple if:

$$\tan\alpha > \frac{8r}{5h}$$

Worked examination question 4 [E]

A uniform right circular cone has height h. The cone is freely hinged at its vertex and is kept in equilibrium by a light rod of length h joining the centre of the base to a point $h\sqrt{3}$ directly above the vertex. Show that the tension in the rod is $Mg\sqrt{3}/4$, where M is the mass of the cone.
Find the magnitude of the reaction at the hinge.

Answer

The first step in a problem of this kind is to draw a clear diagram of reasonable size including all the given information and showing the forces acting.

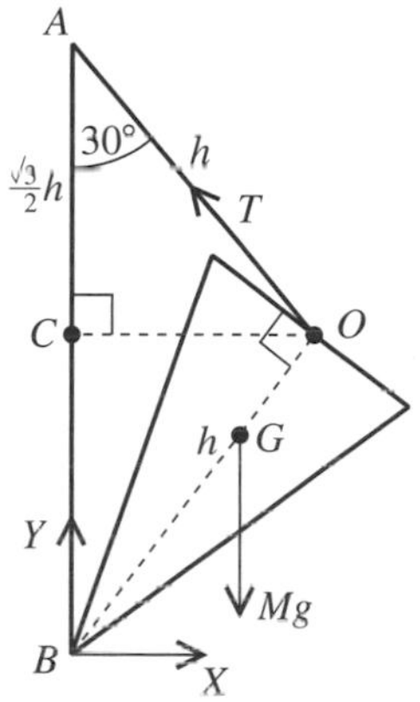

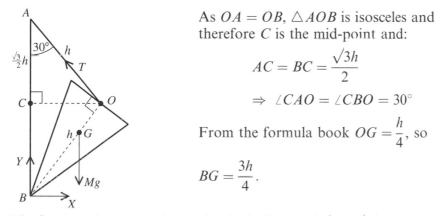

As $OA = OB$, $\triangle AOB$ is isosceles and therefore C is the mid-point and:

$$AC = BC = \frac{\sqrt{3}h}{2}$$

$$\Rightarrow \angle CAO = \angle CBO = 30°$$

From the formula book $OG = \frac{h}{4}$, so

$$BG = \frac{3h}{4}.$$

The forces acting are T, the tension in the light rod, the weight and the reaction at B with horizontal and vertical components X and Y. To find T take moments about B as this will not involve the reaction at B.

Moments ↷: $\quad Mg\left(\frac{3h}{4}\right)\sin 30° - Th\cos 30° = 0$

So: $\quad T = Mg\frac{3h}{4}\frac{1}{h}\tan 30°$

$$= Mg\tfrac{3}{4}\frac{1}{\sqrt{3}} = Mg\frac{\sqrt{3}}{4}$$

To find X and Y resolve horizontally and vertically:
resolving →: $X - T\sin 30° = 0$

so: $\quad X = \frac{Mg\sqrt{3}}{4} \times \frac{1}{2} = Mg\frac{\sqrt{3}}{8}$

resolving ↑: $\quad T\cos 30° + Y - Mg = 0$

so: $\quad Y = Mg - \frac{Mg\sqrt{3}}{4} \times \frac{\sqrt{3}}{2} = \frac{5Mg}{8}$

The magnitude of the reaction is:

$$\sqrt{(X^2 + Y^2)} = Mg\left[\tfrac{3}{64} + \tfrac{25}{64}\right]^{1/2} = Mg\left[\frac{28}{64}\right]^{1/2}$$

$$= Mg\frac{\sqrt{7}}{4}$$

Example 2

A uniform right circular cone has mass M, base radius r and height $4r$. The cone rests in equilibrium on a rough horizontal plane. The coefficient of friction between the cone and the plane is $\frac{3}{4}$. A horizontal force P is applied to the cone half-way up its height.

(a) Find the magnitude of P if the cone is on the point of slipping.

(b) Find the magnitude of P if the cone is on the point of toppling.

(c) If the magnitude of P increases from zero in what way will equilibrium be broken?

Answer

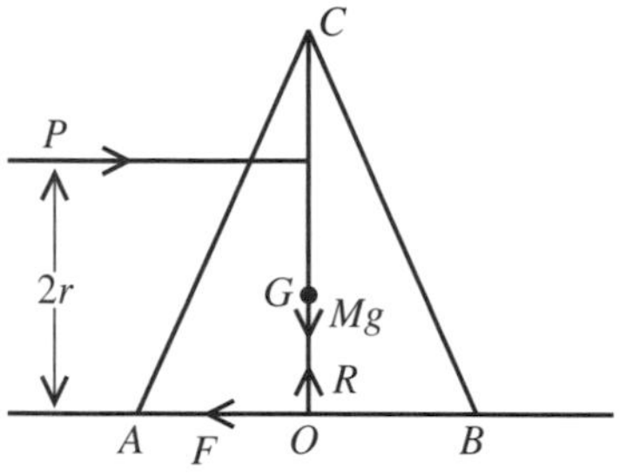

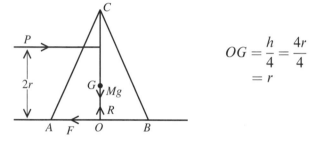

$$OG = \frac{h}{4} = \frac{4r}{4}$$
$$= r$$

From formula book.

Resolving ↑ : $R - Mg = 0$ (1)

Resolving → : $P - F = 0$

If the cone is on the point of slipping:

$$F = \mu R = \tfrac{3}{4}R$$
$$= \tfrac{3}{4}Mg \quad (2)$$

Using (1)

From (2), $P_1 = F = \frac{3}{4}Mg$.

(b) The cone will tilt about the point B.
Taking moments about B:

When tilting takes place, R acts through B and so has no moment about B.

resolving ↷: $P_2 2r - Mgr = 0$

so: $P_2 = \dfrac{Mg}{2}$

(c) As P increases from zero, toppling will occur first since $P_2 < P_1$.

Revision exercise 5

1 A uniform triangular lamina has vertices $A(0, 0)$, $B(4, 0)$ and $C(4, 6)$. Use integration to find the coordinates of the centre of mass of the lamina.

2

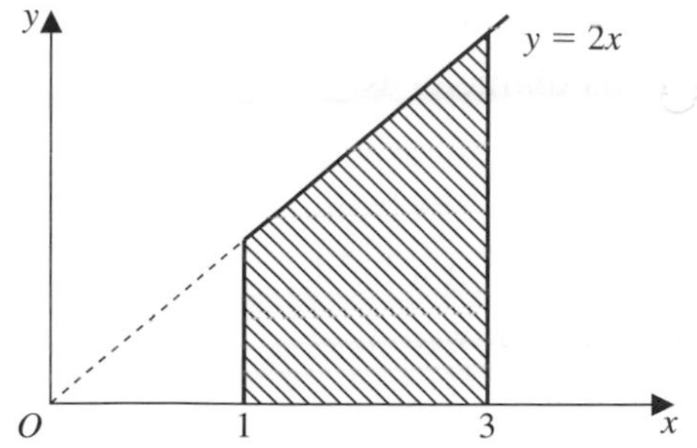

The shaded region in the diagram is bounded by the line $y = 2x$, the lines $x = 1$ and $x = 3$, and the x-axis. This region is rotated completely about the x-axis to give a solid uniform frustrum of a cone, S.

(a) Find the coordinates of the centre of mass of S.

The solid is placed on an inclined plane, rough enough to prevent slipping, with its smaller circular face on the plane. The plane is slowly tilted until the solid is about to topple.

(b) Find the inclination of the plane to the horizontal when the solid topples.

3

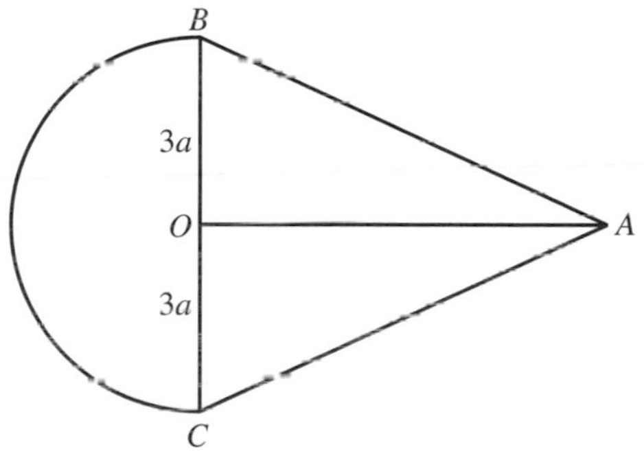

The diagram shows a plane lamina formed by joining a semicircle of radius $3a$ to an isosceles triangle ABC with $AB = AC$ and $OA = x$.

Given that the centre of mass of the lamina is at O, show that $x = 3a\sqrt{2}$.

4 $ABCD$ is a piece of thin plywood of uniform density in the form of a trapezium, BA being parallel to CD and each being perpendicular to BC as shown in the diagram. Given that $AB = a$, $BC = b$ and $CD = c$, find the distances of the centre of mass of the plywood:

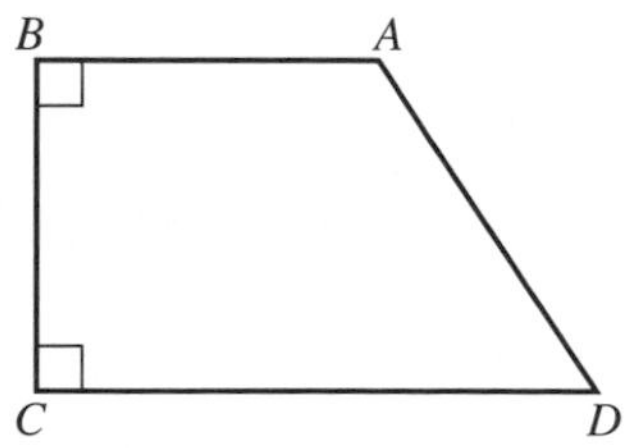

(a) from BC

(b) from AB. [E]

5 A square lamina $ABCD$ of side $2a$ is made of uniform thin metal. When a semicircular piece with CD as diameter is removed from the square, show that the centre of mass of the remainder of the lamina is at a distance $20a/(24 - 3\pi)$ from CD. The remainder of the lamina is suspended from a light string attached at A and hangs in equilibrium. Show that AB is inclined to the downward vertical at an angle θ, where $\tan\theta = \dfrac{(28 - 6\pi)}{(24 - 3\pi)}$.

6 A uniform solid body consists of a hemisphere, a cylinder and a right circular cone, the cone and the hemisphere having the ends of the cylinder as their bases. The radius of the cylinder is three times its length and the height of the cone is equal to the radius of its base. Show that the body can rest in equilibrium with any point of the curved surface of the hemisphere in contact with a horizontal table.

7 **(a)** Show by integration that the centre of mass of a uniform solid hemisphere, of radius R, is at a distance $\frac{3}{8}R$ from its plane face.

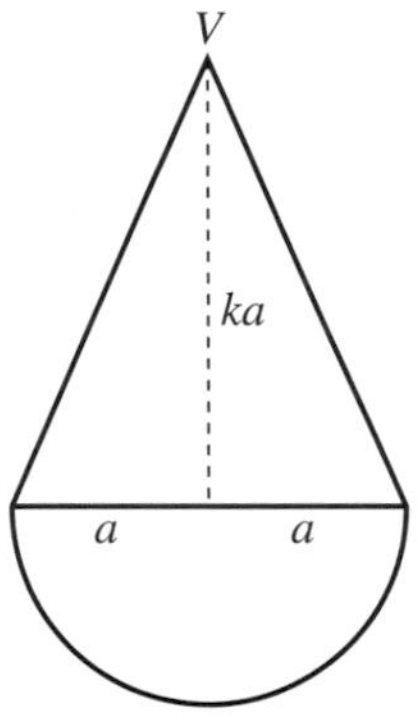

The diagram shows a uniform solid top made from a right circular cone of base radius a and height ka, and a hemisphere of radius a. The circular plane faces of the cone and the hemisphere are coincident.

(b) Show that the distance of the centre of mass of the top from the vertex V of the cone is $\dfrac{(3k^2 + 8k + 3)a}{4(k + 2)}$.

The manufacturer requires the top to have its centre of mass situated at the centre of the coincident plane faces.

(c) Find the value of k for this requirement. [E]

8 A uniform right circular cylinder, of height h and base radius a, is placed with a plane face in contact with a rough plane, the coefficient of friction between the cylinder and the plane being μ. The plane is slowly tilted. Show that the cylinder will topple before it slides if $\mu > 2a/h$.

9 A uniform sphere of radius a has a light inextensible string attached to a point on its surface. The other end of the string is fixed to a point on a rough vertical wall. The sphere rests in equilibrium, touching the wall at a point distant h below the fixed point. The coefficient of friction between the sphere and the wall is μ.
Given that the point of the sphere in contact with the wall is about to slip downwards:
(a) find the inclination of the string to the vertical.

If $\mu = \dfrac{h}{2a}$ and the mass of the sphere is M:

(b) show that the tension in the string is $\dfrac{Mga}{h}\left(1 + \dfrac{h^2}{4a^2}\right)^{\frac{1}{2}}$.

Test yourself

What to review

If your answer is incorrect:

1 **(a)** Use integration to show that the centre of mass of a uniform semicircular lamina, of radius a, is at a distance $\dfrac{4a}{3\pi}$ from O, the mid-point of its straight edge.

Review Heinemann Book M3 page 167 and pages 181–183

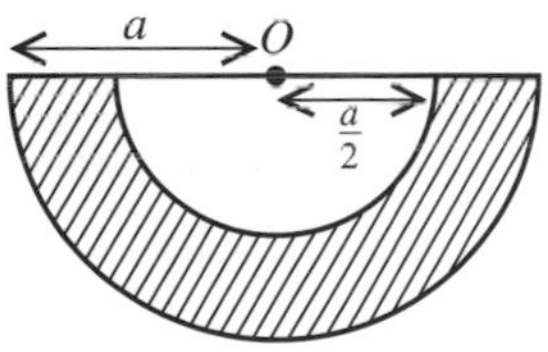

The lamina shown in the diagram is obtained by removing from the lamina in part **(a)** a semicircular lamina of radius $\dfrac{a}{2}$ and with O as the mid-point of its straight edge.
(b) Find the distance of the centre of mass from O.

2

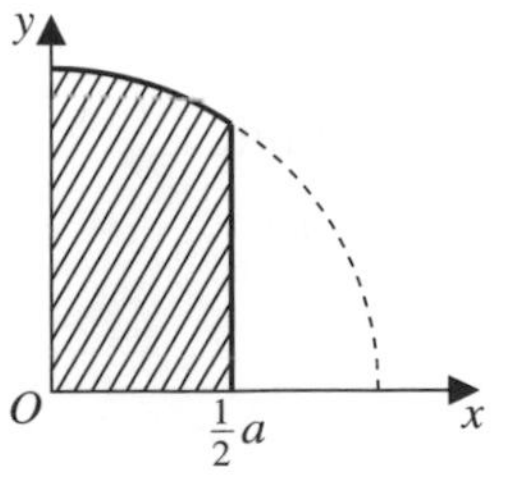

Review Heinemann Book M3 pages 174–175 and pages 185–186

The shaded region in the diagram is bounded by the curve with equation $x^2 + y^2 = a^2$, the lines $x = 0$ and $x = \frac{a}{2}$, and the x-axis. A solid S is formed by rotating this region completely about the x-axis.

(a) Find the coordinates of the centre of mass of S.

The line AB is a diameter of the larger circular face of S. The solid is suspended by a string attached to the point A.

(b) Find the angle made by AB with the downward vertical.

3

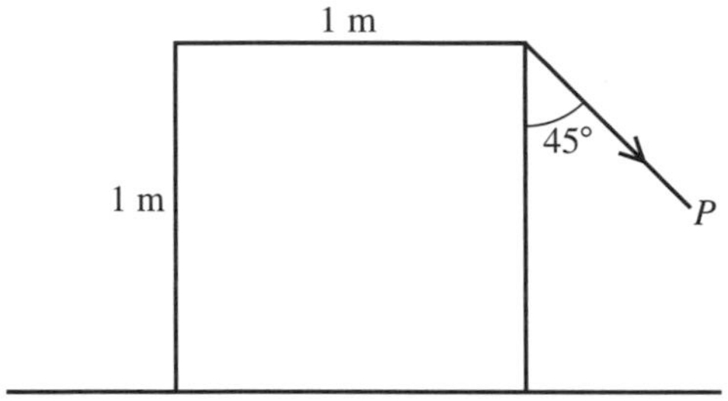

Review Heinemann Book M3 pages 197–202

The diagram shows a square lamina, of side 1 m and mass 4 kg, standing upright on a rough horizontal plane, the coefficient of friction between the lamina and the plane being $\frac{1}{4}$. A string in the vertical plane of the lamina is attached to one corner and makes an angle of 45° with the downward vertical. A force P acts along the string.

(a) Find the magnitude of P if the lamina is on the point of sliding.

(b) Find the magnitude of P if the lamina is on the point of tilting.

The magnitude of P is gradually increased from zero.

(c) Does the lamina slide or topple first?

Test yourself answers

1 (b) $\frac{14a}{9\pi}$

2 (a) $\left(\frac{21a}{88}, 0\right)$ **(b)** 13.4°

3 (a) $\frac{4\sqrt{2}}{3}g$ **(b)** $2\sqrt{2}g$ **(c)** slides first

Examination style paper

Answer all questions **Time allowed: 90 minutes**

1 The non-uniform rod AB is of length L. It hangs in equilibrium suspended from a horizontal ceiling by two vertical elastic strings attached to A and B as shown in the diagram.

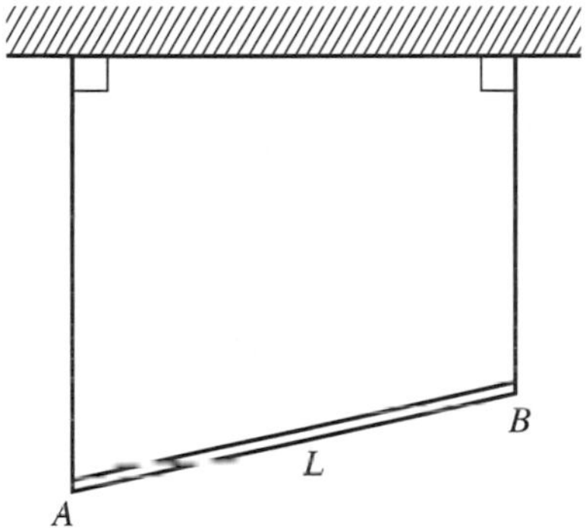

Each of the strings has natural length l and modulus of elasticity λ. The string attached to A has an extension that is twice the extension of the string attached to B.
Find the distance of the centre of mass of the rod from A.
(7 marks)

2 A marble P, of mass m, is moving on the inner surface of a smooth hemispherical bowl with centre O and radius a. The marble is describing a horizontal circle, centre C, with angular speed $\sqrt{\frac{3g}{a}}$. Modelling the marble by a particle find:

(*a*) the magnitude of the force exerted on P by the surface of the bowl **(4 marks)**
(*b*) the depth of C below O. **(4 marks)**

3 A particle P, of mass 0.25 kg, is moving in a straight line on a horizontal plane with simple harmonic motion. P is instantaneously at rest at the points A and B, where $AB = 4$ m, and P travels directly from A to B in 3 seconds.
(*a*) Write down
(i) the amplitude of the motion
(ii) the period of the motion. **(2 marks)**

The mid-point of AB is the point O. The particle reaches the point C 0.5 seconds after it has passed through O.

(b) Find the distance OC. **(4 marks)**

(c) Find, in terms of π, the kinetic energy of P when it is at C. **(4 marks)**

4 A particle P, of mass m, is suspended from a fixed point O by a light elastic string of natural length a and modulus of elasticity $12mg$.

(a) Find the extension in the string when P hangs in equilibrium. **(2 marks)**

The particle is pulled down vertically from its equilibrium position a distance d and released from rest. Given that the particle just reaches O find:

(b) the value of d **(5 marks)**

(c) the maximum speed of P during the motion. **(4 marks)**

5 Bill joins a main road at a speed of $10\,\text{m s}^{-1}$ and accelerates for 20 s to reach a maximum speed of $30\,\text{m s}^{-1}$.

(a) Assuming that the acceleration is constant, estimate the distance travelled by Bill during this 20 second period. **(2 marks)**

Bill found that he had in fact covered a distance greater than the answer found in (a). He therefore considered a refined model in which the acceleration was given by:

$$(\alpha + \beta t)\,\text{m s}^{-2},\ 0 \leqslant t \leqslant 20$$

$$0\,\text{m s}^{-2},\ t \geqslant 20$$

(b) Obtain the values of α and β. **(5 marks)**

(c) Using your values of α and β, obtained in part (b), find a revised estimate for the distance travelled by Bill during this 20 second period. **(4 marks)**

6

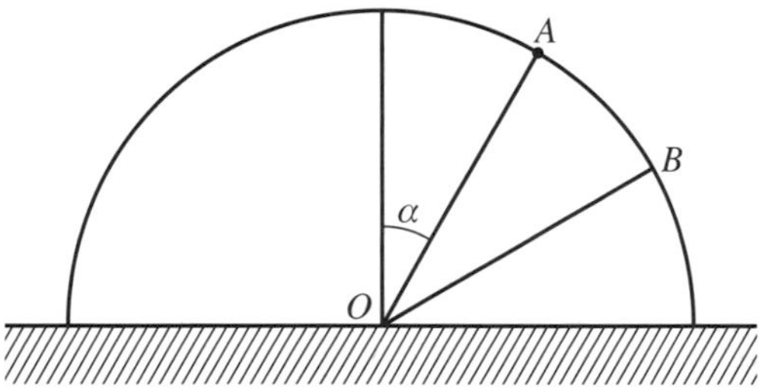

The figure shows a smooth solid hemisphere H, of radius a, fixed with its plane surface, centre O, in contact with horizontal ground. A particle P is released from rest at the point A, on the surface of H, where OA makes an angle $\alpha = \arccos\left(\frac{3}{4}\right)$ with the upward vertical. P slides freely down the hemisphere until it leaves H at the point B with speed v. Given that OB makes an angle β with the upward vertical:

(*a*) show that $\beta = \frac{\pi}{3}$ **(6 marks)**
(*b*) find v^2, in terms of g and a. **(2 marks)**

Given also that the particle strikes the ground with speed V:
(*c*) find V^2, in terms of g and a. **(4 marks)**

7 (*a*) Prove by integration that the centre of mass of a uniform solid right circular cone of height h and base radius r is $\frac{1}{4}h$ from the base of the cone and on the line from the centre of the base to the vertex. **(6 marks)**

A toy is formed by joining such a cone to a uniform solid right circular cylinder, of the same material, with base radius r and length l, so that the plane base of the cone coincides with a plane face of the cylinder, as shown in the figure.

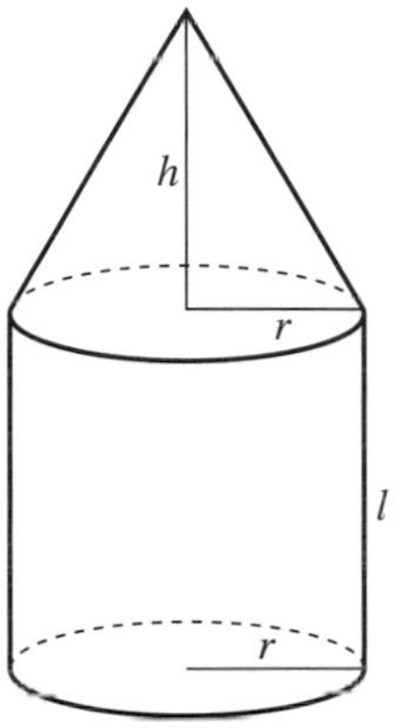

(*b*) Find the position of the centre of mass of the toy. **(5 marks)**

(*c*) Show that, if $6l^2 \geqslant h^2$, this solid can rest in equilibrium on a horizontal plane, with the curved surface of the cylinder touching the plane. **(2 marks)**

Given that $h = 2l$:
(*d*) obtain the condition satisfied by r if the solid can rest in equilibrium with its conical surface touching the plane. **(3 marks)**

Answers

Revision exercise 1

1 **(b)** 117 m
2 **(a)** $2\,\text{m}\,\text{s}^{-1}$ **(b)** $(3 - \text{e})$ m
4 $\sqrt{42}\,\text{m}\,\text{s}^{-1}$ or $6.48\,\text{m}\,\text{s}^{-1}$
5 $k = 2$
6 $v^2 = 36 - 2x^2 - 14x, \quad x = 2$
8 **(a)** $v = \lambda^{\frac{1}{2}}\left(\dfrac{a^4}{x^2} - x^2\right)^{\frac{1}{2}}$ **(c)** $\dfrac{\pi}{(6\sqrt{\lambda})}$

Revision exercise 2

1 98 N
2 0.288 m, 12.3 N
3 $\dfrac{39Mg}{35}$
4 $\lambda_2 = 200g$ N
(a) $18g$ N, $27g$ N **(b)** 0.045 m, B below D
5 **(a)** 10 N **(c)** 1.3
6 $x = \dfrac{2E}{mg}, \ \lambda = \dfrac{m^2g^2l}{2E}$
7 $\frac{2}{3}$m, $\frac{2}{3}$J
8 $\frac{4}{3}a, \ \sqrt{\left(\dfrac{16ga}{3}\right)}$

Revision exercise 3

1 **(a)** $2\mathbf{i} - \text{e}^{-t}\mathbf{j}$ **(b)** 4.32 N
2 **(b)** $v = \sqrt{\left(\dfrac{2gR^2}{X + R} + U^2 - 2gR\right)}$
(c) air resistance
3 **(a)** $v^2 = 8\ln\left(\dfrac{5k}{x + k}\right)$ **(b)** $4m\ln 4$
4 **(b)** 0.4 m **(c)** $0.18\,\text{m}\,\text{s}^{-1}$
5 **(b)** 3.8×10^{-3} N **(c)** 0.34 s
6 **(b)** $\dfrac{\pi}{5}$s
7 **(a)** $\lambda = 2mg$ **(c)** $\pi\sqrt{\dfrac{2l}{g}}$ **(d)** $2l\sqrt{2}$

Revision exercise 4

1 **(a)** 4 N **(b)** $25\,\text{rad}\,\text{s}^{-1}$
2 **(a)** $3mg$ **(b)** $\dfrac{7mg}{3}$
4 **(a)** 21.3 N **(b)** 15.3 m **(c)** $\tan\phi = 3.96$
5 **(a)** $3Mg$ **(b)** $(2\sqrt{2}\,gr)^{\frac{1}{2}}$
7 **(b)** $\frac{3}{16}a$
8 **(b)** 3.7 **(c)** 0.275 m

Revision exercise 5

1 $\left(\frac{8}{3}, 2\right)$
2 **(a)** $\left(2\frac{4}{13}, 0\right)$ **(b)** $\arctan\left(\frac{26}{17}\right) = 56.8°$
4 **(a)** $(a^2 + ac + c^2)/3(a + c)$
(b) $b(a + 2c)/3(a + c)$
7 **(c)** $k = \sqrt{3}$
9 **(a)** $\theta = \text{arcot}\left(\dfrac{h}{a} - \mu\right)$

Examination style paper

1 $\frac{1}{3}L$
2 **(a)** $3mg$ **(b)** $\frac{1}{3}a$
3 **(a)** **(i)** 2 m **(ii)** 6 s
(b) 1 m **(c)** $\dfrac{\pi^2}{24}$
4 **(a)** $\dfrac{a}{12}$ **(b)** $\frac{5}{12}a$ **(c)** $5\sqrt{\dfrac{ag}{12}}$
5 **(a)** 400 m
(b) $\alpha = 2, \ \beta = -\frac{1}{10}$
(c) $466\frac{2}{3}$m
6 **(b)** $v^2 = \frac{1}{2}ga$
(c) $V^2 = \frac{3}{2}ga$
7 **(b)** $\dfrac{6l^2 - h^2}{4h + 12l}$ from common face
(d) $r \geqslant \dfrac{l}{\sqrt{5}}$